EXTENDING
BEYOND
THE PAGES

STANDARDS–BASED
LITERACY LESSONS FOR ANY SUBJECT

INCREASE STUDENT ENGAGEMENT AND
COMPREHENSION BEFORE, DURING,
AND AFTER READING

BY JODIE FRANSEN

IncentivePublications

BY WORLD BOOK
a Scott Fetzer company

Illustrated by Kathleen Bullock
Edited by Marjorie Frank and Kendra Muntz

Acknowledgments
Page 98 "My Teacher Took My iPod" © 2007 by Kenn Nesbitt. Reprinted from "Revenge of the Lunch
Ladies" with the permission of Meadowbrook Press.

Extending Beyond the Pages—Standards-Based Literacy Lessons for Any Subject:
Increase Student Engagement and Comprehension Before, During, and After Reading

Print Edition ISBN 978-1-62950-038-6
E-book Edition ISBN 978-1-62950-039-3 (PDF)

World Book, Inc.
180 North LaSalle Street
Suite 900
Chicago, Illinois 60601
U.S.A.

For information about World Book and Incentive Publications products, call **1-800-967-5325,** or visit
our websites at **www.worldbook.com** and **www.incentivepublications.com.**

Printed in the United States of America by Sheridan Books, Inc.
Chelsea, Michigan
1st printing May 2016

Contents

TAKE IT
BEYOND
THE PAGES

TAKE IT BEYOND THE PAGES

Every text is just words on a page, a screen, or another surface, or the text is read aloud and heard. A text is not alive, not vital—until it connects with or is embraced by a human being! *Extending Beyond the Pages* is about that process—getting texts off the pages (or wherever they might reside) and into the minds and hearts of students. Also, this book is about extending those text connections to deepen understandings of messages from texts students encounter, as well as to help them learn, practice, and polish many literacy skills. The lessons in this book are templates for giving such opportunities to students. Each lesson template can be "laid over" many different texts in many different content areas to inspire engagement with the text and extend—in hundreds of ways—what students can learn from each text.

By the way, throughout this book, the word *text* extends beyond the concept of book pages. It can mean book; chapter; essay; article; excerpt; drama; poem; blog; text message or tweet; advertisement; caption; cartoon; story; movie script; words, images, and messages from a movie or other media presentation; YouTube™ clips; or a host of other ways that words (often accompanied by images) reach your students.

THOUGHTS ON STUDENT CHOICE

I once heard that life could be summed up as one long series of choices. Life-altering, inconsequential, or somewhere in between, the choices we make determine the trajectories of our lives. In every choice there is also a potential lesson to be learned that has the power to influence future choices. If a teacher's job is to help students be successful, contributing members of society, it follows that teachers need to help their students make good choices. Often, however, educators give their students few (or no) choices when it comes to their learning.

There are numerous reasons for this, ranging from state or district mandates to an individual teacher's desire to control all the variables in a classroom. I have found during my 30 years of teaching in the public school system, however, that **giving students choice is one of the best things a teacher can do.** First, it motivates students by giving them a feeling of control. It also enables them to take chances and discover the ways in which they learn best. Additionally, giving students choices helps teachers, too. If students feel they have control over their learning whenever possible, then it's much easier for them to go along with something when it's the teacher's turn to make the choice (e.g., "Now you will all take this required standardized test" or "Yes, you have to give a speech").

Intuitively we, as adults, know this to be true for ourselves as well. The fewer choices we are given, the more resentful we are likely to be and the less likely we are to support those who force decisions upon us. In contrast, when we are given choices, it leads to *thinking*. "Which choice should I make?" "What will happen if I choose…?" "How will my choices affect others?" "What information do I need in making this choice?" Choices can be empowering.

That said, students are works in progress. They don't have the knowledge or life experience to make the right choice all the time, and they cannot be given unlimited choices or the curriculum will never be covered. For that matter, some of them might not show up to school at all if that were an option! So, while choice is crucial, so are guidelines. Give the students choices that you can live with, no matter what they decide. In other words, **the choice isn't "read the book or don't read the book," but rather "choose the book you want to read" and "choose how you want to show that you understood what you read."**

ABOUT THIS BOOK AND HOW TO USE IT

There are 30 lessons in this book. Within each lesson are numerous possibilities for student choice and teacher choice, as well as adaptability for different classes and learning styles. The activities are divided into three categories: **Before Reading, During Reading,** and **After Reading.** It will become apparent, however, that many of these lessons could fit into more than one of these categories and that the categories are mostly for organizational purposes. These lessons also encompass both literature and nonfiction reading skills (as do the standards) and can easily apply to many curricular areas.

Each lesson follows a standard format (described below). Technology connections and arts connections are included for most lessons. However, in some cases, a lesson is primarily a technology activity or an art activity. Or a lesson may not lend itself to technology or art suggestions. In these cases, one of these categories may be omitted from the lesson. Most lessons include student handouts or rubrics to be used as part of the lesson. A few lessons do not need or have any student handouts. In general, the lesson format includes:

- Type of text that can be used for the lesson
- Standards addressed (including specific *Common Core State Standards* numerical identification)
- Approximate lesson time (approximately how long it will take)
- Materials and preparation (what you'll need)
- Overview (a brief look at the lesson's purpose)
- Information for teachers (clarifications and tips)
- Technology connections (ideas for using technology with the lesson)
- Arts connections (ideas for connecting text ideas with various arts)
- Strategies for differentiation (tips for meeting divergent needs in the classroom)
- Assessment (suggestions for ways to assess the learning from the lesson)
- Directions for students (step-by-step process for students to follow)
- Example(s) (samples of student work or student responses for a lesson following the template, or examples of ideas a teacher has used)
- Student handouts and rubrics to use as part of the lesson

TO USE THIS BOOK:

- Choose a lesson that fits your students' needs and the text(s).
- Familiarize yourself with all the components of the lesson.
- Gather materials and prepare any handouts or other features needed.
- Customize any handout templates to fit your students and the text.
- Give students a copy of the "Directions for students" portion of the lesson. (This can be sent electronically or projected for students.)
- Select activities from the ideas listed in the Technology connections, Arts connections, Strategies for differentiation, and Assessment sections.
- Choose and use whatever components of the lesson promise to work best for your students.
- Make an effort to use many different kinds of texts. Sometimes we get stuck on certain genres. Students need to work with all kinds—not the least of which are the kinds they use constantly in their everyday lives.
- Take many opportunities to work with short texts. It is much more effective to teach standards and hone skills with short works than with long ones.

- Include technology use wherever you can and whenever it is appropriate. Always do so within the parameters of your school's policies for technology, Internet use, media use, and such.
- Vary the kinds of activities. Look for opportunities to get students moving, DOING, and collaborating.

In the same way that students need choice—so do teachers! I've tried to create these lessons with much room for adaptation, expansion, combination—whatever it takes for you to take these lessons and make them your own.

TEACHING AND SUPPORTING STANDARDS

The lessons in this book represent my personal teaching philosophy, which is that choices, within guidelines, can give all students the best opportunities to learn. The guidelines, in this case, are the Common Core State Standards (CCSS), which can be further explored at **www.corestandards.org,** or alternatively, the college- and career-ready standards applied in your state or district. These standards provide the framework for learning while allowing much latitude for teachers and students in terms of deciding exactly *how* the learning takes place. Each lesson describes literacy standards they support. Additionally, all lessons are labeled with the CCSS literacy standards they most closely match. See the labels for each lesson and the CCSS-correlation charts on pages 10-17.

FINAL THOUGHTS

The more that you read, the more things you will know.
The more that you learn, the more places you'll go.

~ Dr. Seuss *(I Can Read with My Eyes Shut!)*

In the end, a student's ability to read well enhances everything he or she does. If students engage with the text and each other during the reading process, they will also broaden their literacy skills and be more motivated to read on their own.

It is my hope that these activities will help students do just that: engage. It is the teacher's job to decide which activities work with which texts and which students; there isn't a one-size-fits-all solution. But there is a strategy out there for every student, no matter his or her skill level. With help, all readers can learn to extend beyond the pages and, in the process, learn and grow.

Connections to College- and Career-Readiness Standards for Reading

Common Core Anchor Standards and Grade-Level Standards

Anchor Standard (CCRA) and Related Grade-Level Standards (CCSS)	Standard	Lessons that Support (Section, Lessons)
Key Ideas and Details		
CCRA.R.1 **CCSS: RL.6-8.1;** **RI.6-8.1;** **RH.6-8.1;** **RST.6-8.1**	Read closely to determine what the text says explicitly and to make logical inferences from it; cite specific textual evidence when writing or speaking to support conclusions drawn from the text.	Sec. 1: 1, 2, 3, 4, 6, 8, 10 Sec. 2: 1, 2, 3, 4, 5, 7, 8, 9, 10 Sec. 3: 1, 2, 3, 4, 5, 6, 7, 8, 9, 10
CCRA.R.2 **CCSS: RL.6-8.2;** **RI.6-8.2;** **RH.6-8.2;** **RST.6-8.2**	Determine central ideas or themes of a text and analyze their development; summarize the key supporting details and ideas.	Sec. 1: 1, 2, 3, 4, 8, 10 Sec. 2: 1, 2, 3, 4, 5, 7, 8, 9, 10 Sec. 3: 1, 2, 3, 4, 5, 6, 7, 8, 9, 10
CCRA.R.3 **CCSS: RL.6-8.3;** **RI.6-8.3;** **RH.6-8.3;** **RST.6-8.3**	Analyze how and why individuals, events, and ideas develop and interact over the course of a text.	Sec. 1: 1, 2, 8, 10 Sec. 2: 1, 2, 3, 4, 5, 7, 8, 9, 10 Sec. 3: 1, 2, 3, 4, 5, 6, 7, 8, 9, 10
Craft and Structure		
CCRA.R.4 **CCSS: RL.6-8.4;** **RI.6-8.4;** **RH.6-8.4;** **RST.6-8.4**	Interpret words and phrases as they are used in a text, including determining technical, connotative, and figurative meanings, and analyze how specific word choices shape meaning or tone.	Sec. 1: 3, 4, 10 Sec. 2: 1, 4, 5, 7, 8, 9, 10 Sec. 3: 1, 3, 4, 8, 10
CCRA.R.5 **CCSS: RL.6-8.5;** **RI.6-8.5;** **RH.6-8.5;** **RST.6-8.5**	Analyze the structure of texts, including how specific sentences, paragraphs, and larger portions of the text (e.g., a section, chapter, scene, or stanza) relate to each other and the whole.	Sec. 1: 2, 10 Sec. 2: 2, 4, 5, 7, 9 Sec. 3: 1, 5, 7, 9

Standards for Reading continue on next page.

Anchor Standard and Related Grade-Level Standards	Standard	Lessons that Support (Section, Lessons)
CCRA.R.6 **CCSS: RL.6-8.6;** **RI.6-8.6;** **RH.6-8.6;** **RST.6-8.6**	Assess how point of view or purpose shapes the content and style of a text.	Sec. 1: 10 Sec. 2: 3, 4, 7, 8, 9 Sec. 3: 2, 3, 4, 6, 7, 8, 9, 10
	Integration of Knowledge and Ideas	
CCRA.R.7 **CCSS: RL.6-8.7;** **RI.6-8.7;** **RH.6-8.7;** **RST.6-8.7**	Integrate and evaluate content presented in diverse media and formats, including visually and quantitatively, as well as in words.	Sec. 1: 1, 2, 3, 4, 6, 7, 8, 9, 10 Sec. 2: 1, 2, 3, 4, 5, 7, 8, 9, 10 Sec. 3: 1, 2, 3, 4, 5, 6, 7, 8, 9, 10
CCRA.R.8 **CCSS: RL.6-8.8;** **RI.6-8.8;** **RH.6-8.8;** **RST.6-8.8**	Delineate and evaluate the argument and specific claims in a text, including the validity of the reasoning as well as the relevance and sufficiency of the evidence.	Sec. 1: 7, 8 Sec. 2: 4, 5, 7, 8, 9 Sec. 3: 1, 3, 6, 7, 8, 9
CCRA.R.9 **CCSS: RL.6-8.9;** **RI.6-8.9;** **RH.6-8.9;** **RST.6-8.9**	Analyze how two or more texts address similar themes or topics in order to build knowledge or to compare the approaches the authors take.	Sec. 1: 7, 8 Sec. 2: 9 Sec. 3: 1, 2, 3, 7, 9
	Range of Reading and Level of Text Complexity	
CCRA.R.10 **CCSS: RL.6-8.10;** **RI.6-8.10;** **RH.6-8.10;** **RST.6-8.10**	Read and comprehend complex literary and informational texts independently and proficiently.	Sec. 1: 1, 2, 3, 4, 6, 7, 8, 9, 10 Sec. 2: 1, 2, 3, 4, 5, 7, 8, 9, 10 Sec. 3: 1, 2, 3, 4, 5, 6, 7, 8, 9, 10

Connections to College- and Career-Readiness Standards for Writing

Common Core Anchor Standards and Grade-Level Standards

Anchor Standard and Related Grade-Level Standards	Standard	Lessons that Support (Section, Lessons)
Text Types and Purposes		
CCRA.W.1 **CCSS: W.6-8.1; WHST.6-8.1**	Write arguments to support claims in an analysis of substantive topics or texts, using valid reasoning and relevant and sufficient evidence.	Sec. 2: 9 Sec. 3: 6
CCRA.W.2 **CCSS: W.6-8.2; WHST.6-8.2**	Write informative/explanatory texts to examine and convey complex ideas and information clearly and accurately through the effective selection, organization, and analysis of content.	Sec. 1: 2, 4, 7, 10 Sec. 2: 1, 2, 5, 8 Sec. 3: 3, 6, 7, 8, 9, 10
CCRA.W.3 **CCSS: W.6-8.3; WHST.6-8.3**	Write narratives to develop real or imagined experiences or events using effective technique, well-chosen details, and well-structured event sequences.	Sec. 2: 2, 3 Sec. 3: 2, 8
Production and Distribution of Writing		
CCRA.W.4 **CCSS: W.6-8.4; WHST.6-8.4**	Produce clear and coherent writing in which the development, organization, and style are appropriate to task, purpose, and audience.	Sec. 1: 1, 2, 3, 4, 5, 6, 7, 8, 9, 10 Sec. 2: 1, 2, 3, 4, 5, 7, 8, 9 Sec. 3: 1, 2, 3, 4, 5, 6, 7, 8, 9, 10
CCRA.W.5 **CCSS: W.6-8.5; WHST.6-8.5**	Develop and strengthen writing as needed by planning, revising, editing, rewriting, or trying a new approach.	Sec. 1: 3, Sec. 2: 1, 3, 5, 9, Sec. 3: 8, 10

Standards for Writing continue on next page.

Anchor Standard and Related Grade-Level Standards	Standard	Lessons that Support (Section, Lessons)
CCRA.W.6 **CCSS: W.6-8.6;** **WHST.6-8.6**	Use technology, including the Internet, to produce and publish writing and to interact and collaborate with others.	Sec. 1: 1, 2, 3, 4, 5, 9, 10 Sec. 2: 1, 2, 3, 4, 5, 9, Sec. 3: 1, 3, 4, 5, 6, 7, 8, 9, 10
Research to Build and Present Knowledge		
CCRA.W.7 **CCSS: W.6-8.7;** **WHST.6-8.7**	Conduct short as well as more sustained research projects based on focused questions, demonstrating understanding of the subject under investigation.	Sec. 1: 5, 8, 9 Sec. 2: 2, 3, 4, 9 Sec. 3: 3, 4, 5, 7, 8, 9, 10
CCRA.W.8 **CCSS: W.6-8.8;** **WHST.6-8.8**	Gather relevant information from multiple print and digital sources, assess the credibility and accuracy of each source, and integrate the information while avoiding plagiarism.	Sec. 1: 5, 6, 7, 8, Sec. 2: 2, 3, 4, 9 Sec. 3: 2, 3, 4, 5, 7, 8, 9, 10
CCRA.W.9 **CCSS: W.6-8.9;** **WHST.6-8.9**	Draw evidence from literary or informational texts to support analysis, reflection, and research.	Sec. 1: 1, 2, 3, 4, 5, 7, 8, 9, 10 Sec. 2: 2, 3, 4, 5, 7, 8, 9, 10 Sec. 3: 1, 2, 3, 4, 5, 6, 7, 8, 9, 10
Range of Writing		
CCRA.W.10 **CCSS: W.6-8.10;** **WHST.6-8.10**	Write routinely over extended time frames (time for research, reflection, and revision) and shorter time frames (a single sitting or a day or two) for a range of tasks, purposes, and audiences.	Sec. 1: 1, 2, 3, 4, 5, 6, 9, 7, 8, 10 Sec. 2: 1, 2, 3, 4, 5, 7, 8, 9, 10 Sec. 3: 1, 2, 3, 4, 5, 6, 7, 8, 9, 10

Connections to College- and Career-Readiness Standards for Speaking and Listening

Common Core Anchor Standards and Grade-Level Standards

Anchor Standard and Related Grade-Level Standards	Standard	Lessons that Support (Section, Lessons)
Comprehension and Collaboration		
CCRA.SL.1 **CCSS:** **SL.6-8.1**	Prepare for and participate effectively in a range of conversations and collaborations with diverse partners, building on others' ideas and expressing their own clearly and persuasively.	Sec. 1: 1, 2, 3, 4, 5, 6, 8, 9, 10 Sec. 2: 1, 2, 3, 4, 5, 6, 7, 8, 10 Sec. 3: 1, 2, 3, 4, 6, 9
CCRA.SL.2 **CCSS:** **SL.6-8.2**	Integrate and evaluate information presented in diverse media and formats, including visually, quantitatively, and orally.	Sec. 1: 1, 2, 3, 4, 5, 6, 8, 9, 10 Sec. 2: 1, 2, 3, 4, 5, 6, 7, 8, 10 Sec. 3: 1, 2, 3, 4, 5, 6, 7, 9
CCRA.SL.3 **CCSS:** **SL.6-8.3**	Evaluate a speaker's point of view, reasoning, and use of evidence and rhetoric.	Sec. 1: 5 Sec. 2: 3, 8, 10 Sec. 3: 1, 2, 3, 4, 6, 7, 9

Standards for Speaking and Listening continue on next page.

Connections to CCSS College- and Career-Readiness Standards for Speaking and Listening, continued

Anchor Standard and Related Grade-Level Standards	Standard	Lessons that Support (Section, Lessons)
Presentation of Knowledge and Ideas		
CCRA.SL.4 **CCSS:** **SL.6-8.4**	Present information, findings, and supporting evidence such that listeners can follow the line of reasoning and the organization, development, and style are appropriate to task, purpose, and audience.	Sec. 1: 1, 2, 3, 4, 5, 6, 8, 9, 10 Sec. 2: 1, 2, 3, 5, 6, 7, 8, 10 Sec. 3: 1, 2, 3, 4, 5, 6, 7, 9
CCRA.SL.5 **CCSS:** **SL.6-8.5**	Make strategic use of digital media and visual displays of data to express information and enhance understanding of presentations.	Sec. 1: 1, 2, 6, 9, 10 Sec. 2: 1, 2, 3, 5, 6, 10 Sec. 3: 1, 2, 3, 4, 5, 6, 7, 9
CCRA.SL.6 **CCSS:** **SL.6-8.6**	Adapt speech to a variety of contexts and communicative tasks, demonstrating command of formal English when indicated or appropriate.	Sec. 1: 1, 2, 3, 4, 5, 6, 8, 9, 10 Sec. 2: 1, 2, 3, 4, 5, 6, 7, 8 Sec. 3: 1, 2, 3, 4, 5, 6, 7, 9

Connections to College- and Career-Readiness Standards for Language

Common Core Anchor Standards and Grade-Level Standards

Anchor Standard and Related Grade-Level Standards	Standard	Lessons that Support (Section, Lessons)
Conventions of Standard English		
CCRA.L.1 **CCSS:** **L.6-8.1**	Demonstrate command of the conventions of standard English grammar and usage when writing or speaking.	Sec. 1: 1, 2, 3, 4, 5, 6, 7, 8, 9, 10 Sec. 2: 1, 2, 3, 4, 5, 6, 7, 8, 9, 10 Sec. 3: 1, 2, 3, 4, 5, 6, 7, 8, 9, 10
CCRA.L.2 **CCSS:** **L.6-8.2**	Demonstrate command of the conventions of standard English capitalization, punctuation, and spelling when writing.	Sec. 1: 1, 2, 3, 4, 5, 6, 7, 8, 9, 10 Sec. 2: 1, 2, 3, 4, 5, 6, 7, 8, 9, 10 Sec. 3: 1, 2, 3, 4, 5, 6, 7, 8, 9, 10
Knowledge of Language		
CCRA.L.3 **CCSS:** **L.6-8.3**	Apply knowledge of language to understand how language functions in different contexts, to make effective choices for meaning or style, and to comprehend more fully when reading or listening.	Sec. 1: 1, 3, 4, 5, 6, 7, 8, 9, 10 Sec. 2: 1, 2, 3, 4, 5, 6, 7, 8, 9, 10 Sec. 3: 1, 2, 3, 4, 5, 6, 7, 8, 9, 10

Standards for Language continue on next page.

Connections to CCSS College- and Career-Readiness Standards for Language, continued

Anchor Standard and Related Grade-Level Standards	Standard	Lessons that Support (Section, Lessons)
Vocabulary Acquisition and Use		
CCRA.L.4 **CCSS:** **L.6-8.4**	Determine or clarify the meaning of unknown and multiple-meaning words and phrases by using context clues, analyzing meaningful word parts, and consulting general and specialized reference materials, as appropriate.	Sec. 1: 3, 4, 9, 10 Sec. 2: 1, 4, 5, 6, 9, 10 Sec. 3: 1, 3, 8, 10
CCRA.L.5 **CCSS:** **L.6-8.5**	Demonstrate understanding of figurative language, word relationships, and nuances in word meanings.	Sec. 1: 3, 4, 9, 10 Sec. 2: 1, 9, 10 Sec. 3: 1, 3, 8, 10
CCRA.L.6 **CCSS:** **L.6-8.6**	Acquire and use accurately a range of general academic and domain-specific words and phrases sufficient for reading, writing, speaking, and listening at the college- and career-readiness level; demonstrate independence in gathering vocabulary knowledge when encountering an unknown term important to comprehension or expression.	Sec. 1: 1, 2, 3, 4, 5, 6, 7, 8, 9, 10 Sec. 2: 1, 2, 3, 4, 5, 6, 7, 8, 9, 10 Sec. 3: 1, 2, 3, 4, 5, 6, 7, 8, 9, 10

PART 1
LESSONS
BEFORE
READING

To learn to read is to light a fire;
every syllable that is spelled out is a spark.

~Victor Hugo

Contents

If students are to do any task well, including reading, they need to prepare. The level of preparation needed for reading depends on the length and complexity of the task as well as the amount of background knowledge each student already possesses.

These "Lessons Before Reading" are designed to get students ready to read. They vary from short and simple to extended and complex. Most are easily adaptable to fiction and nonfiction. Some require considerable teacher preparation; others can be done on the spur of the moment. All are aligned to college- and career-readiness literacy standards.

As the teacher, you know best how much preparation is needed for your own students. These tools can help all your students adequately prepare for the tasks ahead. Use each lesson in its briefest form, or develop and extend it to fit the time available and the time your students need.

NOTE: Many of these lessons readily expand into post-reading activities. Revisit the ideas, questions, representations, "noticings," and predictions after the text is read. This will help students integrate all phases of the text examination process (before, during, and after reading). It will also help them compare what they wanted to know to what they learned, what they already knew to what they gained, and what they thought they knew to what turned out to be different.

"I NOTICE ...
I WONDER ..."

Type of text: Literature or informational text

Standards addressed: Standards related to: skimming a text; close examination of key ideas and details; drawing inferences and conclusions; asking questions to learn about texts; using text structure to gain information; integrating and evaluating content; producing clear and coherent writing; gathering relevant information from multiple sources; comprehending orally presented ideas; effectively engaging in collaborations and discussions; presenting knowledge and ideas using multimedia components; conventions of standard English; and knowledge and use of language.

CCSS: ELA-Literacy RL.6-8.1-2, 7, 10; RI.6-8.1-3, 7, 10; RH.6-8.1-2, 7, 10; RST.1-2, 7, 10; W.6-8.4, 6, 9-10; WHST.6-8.4, 6, 9-10; SL.6-8.1-2, 4-6; L.6-8.1-3, 6

Approximate lesson time: 10 to 25 minutes, depending on class size and subject of the lesson

Materials and preparation: Text; copies of student handout "I Notice...I Wonder..." (page 23)

Overview: This basic previewing lesson sharpens skills of observation and skimming, encourages questioning about a text, and enables students to make personal connections with what they're about to read. It also inspires effective engagement in collaborative discussions.

Information for teachers: This lesson can be used to preview any text, group of texts, or unit of study. To introduce the concept, hang two permanent laminated signs (labeled "I notice" and "I wonder") on the wall and refer to them as needed. Use them on the first day of school to open a discussion about what students notice and wonder about the classroom itself. Then use the signs when starting a new text of any kind (including media presentation) or when students are introduced to a new author or begin any other activity.

Technology connections: Ask students to complete the writing as a "group chat" online, on a shared document, on a platform such as Google Classroom™ or Schoology®, or on an electronic bulletin board such as Wallwisher Inc.'s Padlet™.

Arts connections: As an alternative or additional activity, students can create a quick artistic representation of something they noticed. This can involve music, movement, dramatization, photography, drawing, painting, sculpting, etc.

Strategies for differentiation: Students can do this process individually, as partners, or in groups. The writing task can also be completed aloud, on sticky notes, on posters, or online—as fits student needs.

Assessment: As this is an introductory lesson, no formal assessment is appropriate. To encourage student buy-in, it is possible to require each student to participate at least once, give reward points for students who choose to participate, or collect and give points for written work.

Directions for students:

Step 1 **PREVIEW:** Preview the text by scanning it and examining its structure, emphasized phrases or sections, and accompanying graphics.

Step 2 **RECALL:** Recall what you already know about the subject of the text using the prompt "I notice…."

Step 3 **THINK:** Generate questions about the topic using the prompt "I wonder…."

Step 4 **WRITE:** Complete the first three items on the handout.

Step 5 **COLLABORATE:** Share and discuss (in pairs or small groups) what you notice and wonder. The collaborative work can include artistic or technological representations or presentations of what you notice and wonder.

"I Notice . . . I Wonder . . . ," page 3

Example: Students in a large-group setting were asked to orally complete the lesson for the story (and accompanying pictures) "The Tell-Tale Heart," by Edgar Allan Poe.

First, the students flipped through the pages of the text quietly for about twenty seconds.

Then they were asked to share everything they "noticed."
Answers included:

new words

paragraphs

It's not very long for a story.

Next, students shared everything they "wondered."
This time, answers included:

I wonder who the guy in the picture is.

I wonder why the author has three names.

I wonder when this was written.

I wonder what it's about.

I wonder if it's scary.

All the comments were recorded on the board, and then the class read the story. Answers were saved throughout the day so students could compare their reactions to those of students in other classes.

"I Notice . . . I Wonder . . ."

Title of what I'm previewing _____

Previewing the material will help you get ready to read and interact with the new text while you're reading. Use this form to tell what you "notice" and what you "wonder" before you read.

(To *interact with the text* means to closely examine, analyze, evaluate, understand, make connections with, or respond to the text.)

Student Handout

Three things **I notice** are... _____

_____

_____

Three things **I wonder** are... _____

_____

_____

When you're finished reading, put a star by any of your "I wonder" items that were answered in the text.

In the space below, write anything from your "I wonder" list that needs further research:

Name _____ Date _____

INFORMED PREDICTIONS

Type of text: Literature or informational text

Standards addressed: Standards related to: skimming a text; close examination of key ideas and details; making predictions; inferring; citing textual evidence to support predictions; integrating and evaluating content; writing explanatory text; producing clear and coherent writing; gathering relevant information from multiple sources; effectively engaging in collaborations and discussions; presenting knowledge and ideas using multimedia components; conventions of standard English; and knowledge and use of language.

CCSS: ELA-Literacy RL.6-8.1-3, 5, 7, 10; RI.6-8.1-3, 5, 7, 10; RH.6-8.1-3, 5, 7, 10; RST.6-8.1-3, 5, 7, 10; W.6-8.2, 4, 6, 9-10; WHST.6-8.2, 4, 6, 9-10; SL.6-8.1-2, 4, 6; L.6-8.1-3, 6

Approximate time: 30 minutes

Materials and preparation: Text; copies of student handout "My Predictions" for literary text or for informational text (pages 27 and 28)

Overview: This pre-reading lesson engages students in making predictions and inferences while requiring them to cite textual evidence to support their ideas. These predictions will also help the students engage more fully with the text when they read the material.

Information for teachers: Use an entire text or choose small pieces of text on which students base their predictions—for example, the title or a specific passage or page. Assume that students have little or no familiarity with the text before they begin. Students may make predictions individually, in small groups, or as part of a large-group discussion. The handouts are optional; predictions may be made more informally. Record and save the predictions so that students can check their accuracy after the reading is completed.

Technology connections: The handout can easily be completed online (but it should be done individually). Or, students can share their predictions in forms other than the handout. For example, students can share predictions with a text, tweet, group chat, class website (using a platform such as Google Classroom™ or Schoology® chat board), or a Pinterest® board set up by the teacher.

Strategies for differentiation: In this lesson, the differentiation occurs via the text choice. If students are reading books appropriate for their own reading levels, they will be able to make predictions.

Assessment: Assess students on completion of the student handouts (page 27 and 28) with emphasis on the *evidence* matching the predictions (not necessarily the accuracy of the predictions at this point, but rather the students' ability to back up their predictions). See student samples on page 26.

Directions for students:

Step 1 **PREVIEW:** Preview the text you are given.

Step 2 **THINK:** Think about the text and what it could mean, recognizing that, as of yet, you have little or no context or background information.

Step 3 **PREDICT:** Predict what the text is about, what features it might have, and what might happen.

Step 4 **WRITE:** Record your predictions as well as your evidence on one of the "Predictions" student pages (for literary text or informational text). If you are working with a group, complete the prediction handout without talking to other group members.

Step 5 **SHARE:** Share your predictions orally with your group or class.

Informed Predictions, page 3

Examples:

These samples show examples of student predictions. The teacher saved the sheets and gave them back to the students at end of the unit so they could check the accuracy of their predictions.

My Predictions for a Literary Text

Text title and author __*Replay* by Sharon Creech__

Student Handout

Use the sentence starter to make a specific prediction about what you're going to read. In the second sentence, give evidence or reasons for your prediction.

1. I predict that one setting of this text is ... *a theater*

   One piece of evidence that supports this prediction is ... *there is a picture of tickets on the cover and they say, "Admit one."*

2. Three things I predict about the main character are ... *he gets picked on a lot; he's in a school play; he has a good relationship with his father.*

   The evidence that supports these predictions is ... *his name is Leo but everyone calls him Sardine; there are scripts in the book and the cover has theater tickets; there are several chapters in the book that include "Papa" in the title.*

3. One thing I think will happen in the text is ... *Leo will learn something about life from being in a play.*

   The evidence that supports this prediction is ... *It makes sense because he's the main character and most stories have some sort of lesson about life.*

4. After reading the text, highlight the aspects of your prediction that were correct or nearly correct.

   Name _____ Date _____

My Predictions for an Informational Text

Text title and author __From the online article called "The Building of the First Theater in England" written in 1904__

Source __Mantzius, Karl. "Building of the First Theatre in England" AD. 1576. The Great Events by Famous Historians. Vol 10. Harrogate TN: The National Alumni. 1926. Web. 11 July 2015__

Student Handout

Use the sentence starter to make a specific prediction about what you're going to read. In the second sentence, give evidence or reasons for your prediction.

1. I predict that one major topic this text will cover is ... *the building of the Globe Theater*

   One piece of evidence that supports this prediction is ... *there is a summary at the beginning that mentions the Globe, and I know from history that this was an early English theater.*

2. I predict that this text will answer a question I have about ... *when actors started putting on plays in England.*

   The evidence that supports this prediction is ... *the title; and by skimming the article I see it has lots of good historical information.*

3. One thing I want to learn from this text is ... *what kind of plays used to be presented and what it was like to be in a play in the 1500's.*

4. After reading the text, highlight the aspects of your prediction that were correct or nearly correct

   Name _____
   Date _____

My Predictions for a Literary Text

Text title and author _____

Use the sentence starter to make a specific prediction about what you're going to read. In the second sentence, give evidence or reasons for your prediction.

Student
Handout

1. I predict that one setting of this text is

    One piece of evidence that supports this prediction is

2. Three things I predict about the main character are

    The evidence that supports these predictions is

3. One thing I think will happen in the text is

    The evidence that supports this prediction is

4. After reading the text, highlight the aspects of your prediction that were correct or nearly correct.

Name _____ Date _____

My Predictions for an Informational Text

Text title and author _____

Source _____

Use the sentence starter to make a specific prediction about what you're going to read. In the second sentence, give evidence or reasons for your prediction.

Student Handout

1. I predict that one major topic this text will cover is

   One piece of evidence that supports this prediction is

2. I predict that this text will answer a question I have about

   The evidence that supports this prediction is

3. One thing I want to learn from this text is

4. After reading the text, highlight the aspects of your prediction that were correct or nearly correct

Name _____ Date _____

RANDOM WORD PULL

Type of text: Literature or informational text

Standards addressed: Standards related to: skimming a text; close examination of key ideas and details; drawing inferences and conclusions; integration of content presented in diverse formats; acquiring and using vocabulary; determining meanings of words and phrases as they are used in a text; producing clear and coherent writing; effectively engaging in collaborations and discussions; presenting knowledge and ideas using a variety of components, including the arts and technology; conventions of standard English; and knowledge and use of language.

CCSS: ELA-Literacy-RL.6-8.1-2, 4, 7, 10; RI.6-8.1-2, 4, 7, 10; RH.6-8.1-2, 4, 7, 10; RST.6-8.1-2, 4, 7, 10; W.6-8.4, 6, 9-10; WHST.6-8.4, 6, 9-10; SL.6-8.1-2, 4-6; L.6-8.1-6

Approximate time: 50 minutes as written, but easily shortened by combining student steps 2 and 3 so that groups work together to choose a total of about six words

Materials and preparation: Text; copies of student handouts "Random Word Pull" (page 32) and "Random Word Pull Rubric" (page 33); dictionary

Overview: This lesson is designed to preview a text while reinforcing and teaching vocabulary. It also gives students opportunities to become intrigued with words, use resources to find word meanings, write about the words, demonstrate and otherwise communicate understandings of words, and collaborate with peers about word meanings and uses.

Information for teachers: This can be used prior to beginning a new unit or a single text. It is a good way to generate vocabulary that students are interested in learning, and these words can also be used in other vocabulary activities. Let students work in groups of four or five.

Technology connections: Students can use online texts and resources to find word meanings. Groups can also put their answers on an electronic document rather than on a handout.

Strategies for differentiation: Students with lower or higher reading abilities can use different texts. Groups may also be formed in such a way that students with similar abilities work together. Alternatively, groups can be formed with students of different levels working together so that more advanced students can help those who may struggle. Since the students are looking for their own words, differentiation will also occur naturally as students search for words that interest them personally.

Assessment: Groups or individuals can be assessed on their ability to work together as well as the accuracy of their handouts. A rubric is included. (See page 33.) The teacher and the individual student or group can assess the work with this rubric.

Directions for students:

Step 1   **SKIM:** Skim through the assigned page(s), looking for words that may be interesting or unfamiliar.

Step 2   **WRITE:** Choose three words you like the best and write them at the top of the handout "Random Word Pull."

Step 3   **SHARE:** Have every person in your group share his or her favorite words. After sharing, each student chooses one word and one student in the group writes them all on the handout. Be sure there are no repeats.

Step 4   **WRITE:** On the handout, write each word's part of speech and definition as used in the text.

Step 5   **PRESENT:** Draw, diagram, act out, advertise on a poster or with a presentation software program the meanings of the words.

Example: Students were preparing to research the concept of plate tectonics in a science class. They were going to begin by reading an online article about the topic (Cloos, Mark. "Plate tectonics." *World Book Student.* World Book, 2014. Web. 28 June 2014).

- As this text is from an electronic source, it was easy for students to scan the entire article looking for new words. They were also encouraged to use the table of contents to give them an overview before they began.

- All students completed the handout on their own, discovering such words as:

supercontinent	*lithosphere*	*outermost*	*convergent*
Pangaea	*divergent*	*embedded*	*subsection*
mantle	*rift*	*subduction*	*accretion*

- Since each group had five students, each group chose five words total from all the lists and wrote them in the chart on the handout.

- Groups then used an online dictionary to find each term's part of speech (as it was used in the article) as well as its definition. The teacher was available to help students with content-specific words that may be harder to understand.

- Students went on to draw, diagram, or demonstrate the word meanings.

- As a follow-up, the science teacher shared the students' word list with their language arts teacher. He kept the list visible and reinforced students' abilities to show understanding of and fluency with the words.

Random Word Pull

1. Use this space to write at least 10 interesting and/or unfamiliar words you see in the text:

Student Handout

2. Share your words with your group. Then together choose the group's five favorites from each group member's words and write them in the first column below.

3. Next, use a dictionary to fill in the correct part of speech and a short definition that matches the way the word is used in the text.

4. Then find a way to show that you understand the words—with cartoons, drawings, diagrams, or demonstrations.

Word	Part of Speech	Definition
1.		
2.		
3.		
4.		
5.		

Name _____   Date _____

Random Word Pull Rubric

Student Handout

Scoring Guide:

4 = **Advanced** = exceeds requirements

3 = **Proficient** = meets requirements

2 = **Partially Proficient** = meets some but not all requirements

1 = **Unsatisfactory** = meets less than 50% of requirements

Skill	Description	Self or Group Score (1-4)	Teacher Score (1-4)	Teacher Comments
Collaboration	Engages effectively in conversation and collaboration with group; expresses ideas and builds on others' ideas.			
Word Choice	Chooses precise and varied vocabulary words from the selection.			
Research	Consults reference materials to determine or clarify precise meanings of words as used in context.			
Accuracy	Writes the correct meanings of words as they are used in the text, including technical meanings when needed.			

Name _____ Date _____

VOCABULARY PREVIEW

Type of text: Literature or informational text

Standards addressed: Standards related to: skimming a text; close examination of key ideas and details; drawing inferences and conclusions; determining meanings of words and phrases as they are used in a text; acquiring and using vocabulary; writing explanatory text; producing clear and coherent writing; effectively engaging in collaborations and discussions; presenting knowledge and ideas using a variety of components, including the arts and technology; conventions of standard English; and knowledge and use of language.

CCSS: ELA-Literacy-RL.6-8.1-2, 4, 7, 10; RI.6-8.1-2, 4, 7, 10; RH.6-8.1-2, 4, 7, 10; RST.6-8.1-2, 4, 7, 10; W.6-8.2, 4, 6, 9-10; WHST.6-8.2, 4, 6, 9-10; SL.6-8.1-2, 4-6; L.6-8.1-6

Approximate time: 40 minutes

Materials and preparation: Copies of teacher-generated vocabulary list (see template on page 37); copies of "Vocabulary Preview Rubric" (page 38)

Overview: This lesson is designed to familiarize and intrigue students with critical vocabulary words prior to reading. It also gives students opportunities to use resources to find word meanings, demonstrate or communicate understandings of words, and collaborate with peers about word meanings.

Information for teachers: In contrast to the "Random Word Pull" lesson, the teacher chooses the words and students explore the meanings before they read the text. Insert your words into column 1 of the handout. Note the part of speech as the word is used in the text and the page or stanza number where the word is located in the text. Students read the text after they have found definitions and discussed the words. After that, they can go back to their definitions to see if any need to be adjusted based on the context.

Technology connections: Students can use computers to find definitions and examples as well as a copy of the text, for example, a poem. Using an online audio book can also be helpful to give students the flow and rhythm of the text.

Arts connections: Students may choose a portion from the text and express it in a drawing or painting. Students can also be asked to set the text to music or to choose a popular song that they feel would make suitable background music for this text.

Strategies for differentiation: After choosing the words you will use, list them in order of increasing difficulty. Then the assignment can be modified for the students (e.g., students who work more slowly or who have reading difficulties can do only the first five, etc.).

Assessment: Students or the teacher can use the rubric on page 38 to assess student performance and understanding.

Directions for students:

Step 1   **READ and THINK:** Read through the given words. Think about them and whether or not you already know their definitions.

Step 2   **WRITE:** On the handout, "Vocabulary Preview," write the given words in the first column.

Step 3   **RESEARCH:** Look up each word in a dictionary. If a word has multiple definitions, use the context of the word (the words before and after the word) or its part of speech to help you choose the correct one.

Step 4   **WRITE:** Write each word's definition on the handout. Then write a complete sentence that uses the word correctly.

Step 5   **PRESENT:** Explain, draw, act out, or demonstrate the meaning of the words and discuss them with classmates.

Step 6   **READ:** When you read the text, keep your handout nearby. See if your definitions work in the actual context of your text.

Example: This example is based on student reading of Edgar Allan Poe's poem "Annabelle Lee."

Before reading Edgar Allan Poe's poem "Annabelle Lee," students completed the student handout (page 37) on which the teacher had listed these words:

seraph	coveted	highborn	sounding
kinsman	envying	dissever	sepulchre*

(*This is the British spelling that Poe used. The standard United States spelling is sepulcher.)

Students then shared (in discussion) their word meanings and showed their understandings by representing them with art, drama, or movement.

Their representations included:

- *a role-play (with some helpers) of acts and actions showing* **coveted**
- *a diagram of things at the bottom of a* **sounding** *sea—designed to show the concept of the very deep sea*
- *a group of illustrations of objects that might be owned or used by someone who is* **highborn**
- *a hand-drawn sketch of* **seraphs** *(angels)*
- *a demonstration of situations where some things are* **dissevered**
- *a visual collage of images of* **sepulchres** *(tombs) and words that are synonyms for* **sepulchre**

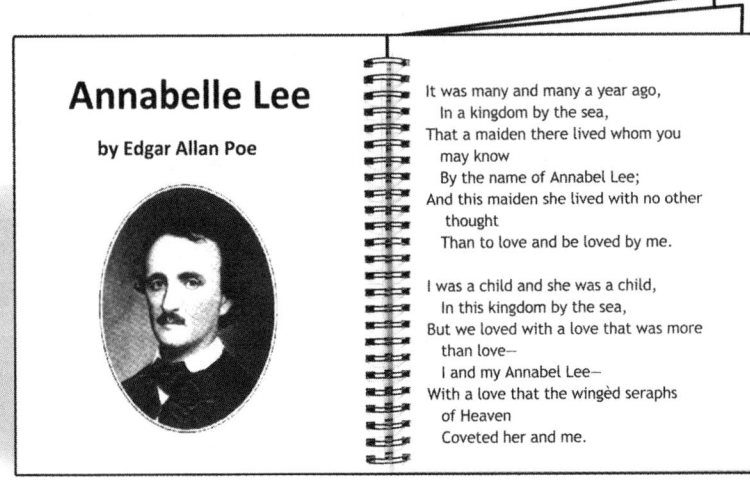

Annabelle Lee

by Edgar Allan Poe

It was many and many a year ago,
  In a kingdom by the sea,
That a maiden there lived whom you
  may know
    By the name of Annabel Lee;
And this maiden she lived with no other
  thought
    Than to love and be loved by me.

I was a child and she was a child,
  In this kingdom by the sea,
But we loved with a love that was more
  than love—
    I and my Annabel Lee—
With a love that the wingèd seraphs
  of Heaven
    Coveted her and me.

Vocabulary Preview

Use the vocabulary list given to you to complete this chart.

Student Handout

Word, Location, Part of Speech	Clear, Concise Definition	The Word Used in a Sentence

Name _____ Date _____

Vocabulary Preview Rubric

Student Handout

Scoring Guide:

4 = **Advanced** = exceeds requirements

3 = **Proficient** = meets requirements

2 = **Partially Proficient** = meets some but not all requirements

1 = **Unsatisfactory** = meets less than 50% of requirements

Skill	Description	Self or Group Score (1-4)	Teacher Score (1-4)	Teacher Comments
Research	Consults reference materials to determine or clarify precise meanings of words as used in context.			
Accuracy	Writes the correct meaning of words as they are used in the text, including technical meanings when needed.			
Sentences	Creates accurate sentences that use the vocabulary words correctly.			

Name _____ Date _____

GOAL-SETTING INTERVIEWS

Type of text: Literature or informational text

Standards addressed: Standards related to: asking questions to gain information; producing clear and coherent writing; strengthening writing; publishing writing; effectively engaging in collaborations and discussions; presenting knowledge and ideas using a variety of components—including the arts and technology; evaluating speaking performance; listening; conventions of standard English; and knowledge and use of language.

CCSS: ELA-Literacy.W.6-8.4-10; SL.6-8.1-4, 6; L.6-8.1-3, 6

Approximate time: 20 minutes for students to prepare plus 20 minutes for interview time and self-reflection

Materials and preparation: Copies of student handouts "Setting Goals for Reading" (page 42) and "Interview Self Evaluation" (page 43); recording tool (camera, tablet, smartphone, etc.)

Overview: This lesson helps students reflect on their reading goals, take responsibility for their reading, and practice listening and speaking skills before reading any text. Recording the interviews improves motivation and accountability.

Information for teachers: Working with a partner, each student will identify reading goals and create questions for his or her partner that encourage the partner to think about his or her reading goals. (They can do this on the "Setting Goals for Reading" student handout [page 42]. When the goal-setting sheets are completed, students will interview each other [while recording their interaction].) The results can be played for the class, evaluated by the teacher, or both. After the lesson, students will complete a self evaluation, reflecting upon their work.

Technology connections: Results will be better if students have external microphones to use. Students can also edit their work on a program such as iMovie® and post their interviews on the class website or a video-sharing site (following your school's guidelines).

Arts connections: Students can create a graphic representation (such as a graphic organizer) on paper or on screen to show their reading goals and keep record of progress toward those goals.

Strategies for differentiation: Students can be given a script to read prior to recording. Students with outstanding computer skills can be in charge of the equipment, the editing, adding music or subtitles, etc.

Assessment: As this is a pre-reading lesson, it is best to assess it as a completion score. (Give a percentage for the amount of the assignment that is completed.) Also, the self evaluation on page 43 will help students assess their own accomplishments. At the end of the year, quarter, or semester, students can do follow-up interviews to ask each other about their goals and whether or not they were achieved.

Directions for students:

Step 1   **PREPARE:** Think about three specific goals you have for yourself as a reader as well as some questions you might ask your partner about reading.

Step 2   **THINK:** Fill out the pre-interview handout, "Setting Goals for Reading."

Step 3   **INTERVIEW:** Interview your partner while you are being recorded. Then trade and have your partner interview you.

Step 4   **WATCH and REFLECT:** Watch your interview and reflect on how it went. Think about yourself as a speaker and a listener.

Example:  Here is an example of a student's self evaluation on the goal-setting and interview experience. These are her responses from the "Interview Self Evaluation" student page:

1. One thing I noticed about our interview was... *we both had some of the same goals and it was hard to be recorded without laughing!*

2. One thing about our interview that I'm proud of is... *we took it seriously and answered all of each other's questions.*

3. Two things I'd like to change or do differently are... *I should have worn something else because I looked weird. Also, I would change some of my strategies for meeting my goals.*

4. When it was my turn to ask the questions, I noticed... *I stumbled on a few words but I had some good questions to ask and they made my partner think about his reading.*

5. When it was my turn to listen, I noticed... *my partner asked good questions and made me think about myself as a reader.*

6. Here are some ways this assignment contributed to my goals for myself as a reader, or some things I learned from the interview process: *The recording was fun and gave us a chance to go back later and see if we did what we said we were going to do. I liked creating my own questions. It helped me think seriously about my own reading goals and learn something about my partner. Now we can help each other in reaching our goals.*

Setting Goals for Reading

Fill this sheet out prior to your interview.

1. One goal I have for my reading is . . .

One thing I can do to reach this goal is . . .

2. Another goal I have for my reading is . . .

One thing I can do to reach this goal is . . .

3. Three questions I can ask my partner about his/her reading are:

I.

II.

III.

Interview directions:

- Set up the camera so both of you are in the picture. Decide who will be Partner 1 and Partner 2. Partner 1 begins, asking Partner 2 to share his or her two goals and ideas for reaching them. When Partner 2 finishes, switch roles.

- Next, Partner 1 asks the questions he or she prepared. When Partner 2 is done answering, switch roles.

- When you're all done, turn off the camera and watch the interviews. Then fill out the "Interview Self Evaluation" (page 43).

Name _____ Date _____

Interview Self Evaluation

1. One thing I noticed about our interview was . . .

2. One thing about our interview that I'm proud of is . . .

Student Handout

3. One thing I'd like to change or do differently is . . .

4. When it was my turn to ask the questions, I noticed . . .

5. When it was my turn to listen, I noticed . . .

6. Here are some ways this assignment contributed to my goals for myself as a reader, or some things I learned from the interview process:

Name _____ Date _____

THE GALLERY WALK

Type of text: Literature or informational text

Standards addressed: Standards related to: asking questions to gain information; integrating visual information with print or digital text information; producing clear and coherent writing; effectively engaging in collaborations and discussions; conventions of standard English; and knowledge and use of language.

CCSS: ELA-Literacy.RL.6-8.1, 7, 10; RI.6-8.1, 7, 10; RH.6-8.1, 7, 10; RST.6-8. 1, 7, 10; W.6-8.4, 8, 10; WHST.6-8.4, 8, 10; SL.6-8.1-2, 4-6; L.6-8.1-3, 6

Approximate time: 40 minutes (excluding teacher preparation)

Materials and preparation: Printed pictures and artwork to hang on the wall. (These can include pictures of anything related to the text students will read, i.e., setting, characters, historical context, topics, details; the works of art may include captions); sticky notes for students to write questions

Overview: This lesson is designed to give students a visual reference prior to reading a text and generate interest in the text. It also involves movement and active participation and encourages students to ask questions prior to reading.

Information for teachers: For this lesson, you will need to create a gallery of photographs that relate to the text the students will be reading. This works well with novels or complex stories that have multiple layers and components. It is also very effective with historical fiction. (See example on page 46.) It can also work with a variety of nonfiction, informational topics.

Arts connections: At its core, this is an art-based lesson. Consult your art specialist and ask him or her to give the students more understanding of appreciating photographs and art. Also, to add an additional sensory layer, appropriate music can be played during the gallery walk.

Strategies for differentiation: By choosing a wide variety of pictures to display, students will be able to differentiate for themselves by choosing what appeals to them and what they are able to understand in the works of art.

Assessment: This lesson is based on participation, so formal assessment is not appropriate. One way to add accountability is to give each student a specific number of sticky notes, 10, say, and require the students to use them all during the gallery walk. If needed, students can be assessed on the number and quality of their questions as well as their participation in the lesson and in the discussion that follows.

Directions for students:

Step 1 **WALK and OBSERVE:** Silently walk around the room and view the photographs and other images. Spend at least a minute at each one, paying attention to details.

Step 2 **WRITE:** At each picture, write a question on a sticky note and place it under the picture. The question can be about anything that relates to the picture or your reaction to it.

Step 3 **WRITE:** Take some brief notes on each image so that you can remember it as well as your thoughts and questions about it.

Step 4 **DISCUSS:** Meet with two or three classmates to share your observations and questions about the images in the gallery.

Example:  In a Social Studies class, eighth-grade students participated in a gallery walk prior to reading *No Promises in the Wind* (Hunt, 1970). This book is historical fiction set in the 1930's, so photographs included the following:

- Depression-era photos, including "bread lines," foreclosures, dust-laden fields

- Photos related to the plot and specific settings of the story, including freight trains, traveling carnivals, and the city of Chicago

- Photos related to the characters, including families with two sons, single mothers, and people with dwarfism

---

Here are some of the questions generated by the students:

- *Who rode on the trains?*

- *Why did all the crops die?*

- *Did they have single moms in the 1930's?*

- *Is this all one big family?*

- *What kinds of jobs did these men do?*

- *Did they really have blue jeans back then?*

- *Why did all the girls wear dresses?*

- *Why did people lose their houses?*

- *Where did the carnivals travel?*

- *Who worked in the carnivals?*

- *How did people survive this?*

- *Were the trains safe?*

- *What effects did the carnival life have on families?*

- *How did people end up having to stand in lines for food?*

AUTHOR VIDEOS

Type of text: Literature or informational text or group of texts by one author

Standards addressed: Standards related to: comprehending information presented in various formats, including multimedia formats; integrating previous knowledge with new texts; asking questions to acquire information; summarizing; listening; integrating visual information with print or digital text information; writing informational text; producing clear and coherent writing; conventions of standard English; and knowledge and use of language.

CCSS: ELA-Literacy. RL.6-8.7-8, 10; RI.6-8.7-8, 10; RH.6-8.7-8, 10; RST.6-8, 7-8, 10; W.6-8.2, 4, 8-10; WHST.6-8.2, 4, 8-10; SL.6-8.1-2; L.6-8.1-3, 6

Approximate time: About 40 to 60 minutes (depending on the video length) plus time for pre- and post-activities

Materials and preparation: Video; copies of teacher-prepared notes on the author of a text or texts students will read (use the student handout template "Video Notes" on page 50); quiz on video information (optional)

Overview: Watching a video about a specific author helps students make visual, auditory, and historical connections with a text prior to reading.

Information for teachers: Many good videos are available that have biographical sketches of authors. Choose a video on an author of a text or group of texts students will read. Rather than simply show the video, balance scaffolding with student independence by presenting students with a few notes prior to the video. This gives them enough background to understand what they are seeing while allowing them to fill in their own facts and summary. As you create the "Video Notes" handout, leave space for students to add notes and questions. (See page 50 for handout template.)

Arts connections: Play music from an author's culture to enhance the experience. Have students draw pictures or make collages of the author's life and works.

Strategies for differentiation: If a student has difficulty with note taking, pair him or her with another student who is taking notes. After viewing the video, allow time for the pair to discuss the notes briefly and for the student who struggled with the note-taking task to write some notes.

Assessment: Before students watch the video, tell them that they'll be taking an open-note quiz on the information they see and hear. This will encourage attentiveness to the video and thoughtful note taking.

Directions for students:

Step 1 **PREVIEW:** Review the notes presented to you on the handout, "Video Notes." Jot down anything you already know or have heard about this author.

Step 2 **WATCH and LISTEN:** Watch the video about the author and his or her circumstances.

Step 3 **WRITE:** Add to the notes as you watch. Write other important facts or ideas you hear.

Step 4 **SUMMARIZE:** Write a summary of the key ideas you learned from the video.

Step 5 **THINK:** Use your new background knowledge of the author to help you understand the texts you read by that author.

Example: Prior to her students watching a video, *Edgar Allan Poe: Terror of the Soul*, a teacher presented them with "Video Notes" including such information as:

1. Background information

- *American writer who lived from 1809 to 1849*
- *Wrote more than 70 stories, plus articles, poems, reviews, a novella (short novel), and part of a play*
- *Much of his life is a mystery because many critics didn't like him personally and slandered him after his death. (**Slander** is false accusations or stories that harm someone's reputation.)*

2. Poems and stories mentioned or dramatized in the video:

- *"The Tell-Tale Heart"*
- *"The Raven"*
- *"The Black Cat"*
- *"The Pit and the Pendulum"*
- *"The Fall of the House of Usher"*
- *"The Cask of Amontillado"*

Example: Students watched a video on Mark Twain. The teacher gave a quiz after the viewing to check comprehension of details. Here are some sample questions:

- *Mark Twain's real name was:*
  a. *Edgar Poe*
  b. *Clement Adler*
  c. *Samuel Langdon*
  d. *Samuel Clemens*

- *For which of the following writing techniques is Twain NOT known?*
  a. *humor*
  b. *allegory*
  c. *exaggeration*
  d. *satire*

- *Which job did Twain NEVER have?*
  a. *painter*
  b. *writer*
  c. *riverboat pilot*
  d. *newspaper editor*

- *Mark Twain wrote*
  a. *novels*
  b. *short stories*
  c. *essays*
  d. *all of the above*

Video Notes

Author _____

Name of text(s) you will read _____

Review this information. As you watch the video, add notes.

I. Background information

Student Handout

II. Titles of other texts mentioned in the video

III. Questions you would like to ask about this author

IV. Summary—On the back of this page, briefly summarize the key ideas or information you learned about this author.

Name _____ Date _____

SLIDE SHOW PREVIEW

Type of text: Literature or informational text

Standards addressed: Standards related to: reading and comprehending information presented in various formats, comparing and contrasting written text to audio or visual presentations including multimedia formats; asking questions to acquire information; listening; integrating visual information with print or digital text information; producing clear and coherent writing; effectively engaging in collaborations and discussions; conventions of standard English; and knowledge and use of language.

CCSS: ELA-Literacy. RL.6-8.1-3, 7-10; RI.6-8.1-3, 7-10; RH.6-8.1-3, 7-10; RST.6-8.1-3, 7-10; W.6-8.4, 7-10; WHST.6-8.4, 7-10; SL.6-8.1-2, 4, 6; L.6-8.1-3, 6

Approximate time: 30 to 40 minutes (excluding teacher preparation)

Materials and preparation: Collection of appropriate pictures, art, and quotations related to a text students will read; copies of student handout "Slide Show Preview" (page 54); technology for presentation (computer, projector)

Overview: This lesson helps visually oriented students make connections with different aspects of the text they're about to read and deepens understanding of the text topic for all students.

Information for teachers: Collect pictures, cartoons, quotations, primary documents, and short video clips and compile them using a program such as PowerPoint®, Keynote®, or Google Slides™. Make each "slide" a unique item. Include numbers on the slides as a guide for students. For the lesson, show each slide for a specific time period (90 seconds works well) and have the students record their thoughts on the handout. This can be done as a quiet reflective activity or a more interactive activity (with discussions before, during, or after the slides) depending on the subject matter. The handout template on page 54 includes spaces for six slides but is easily adapted to fewer or more.

Technology connections: Try having students complete the response to the slides as a "group chat" online or in a digital document.

Arts connections: To deepen the arts connection at the heart of this lesson, students can respond with images or slides with visual ideas they create or find in classroom resources (including on the Internet). Or they can portray the idea in a slide through other means of expression, such as music or movement.

Strategies for differentiation: As accepted responses will vary widely, this lesson reaches all levels of students. The slide show can easily be adapted to any level. Students who struggle with writing can give oral responses. Higher-ability students can be asked to make slides to add to the show.

Assessment: Students should be assessed on participation and thoughtful responses rather than "correctness." Collect the handout from each student and assign points to each item.

Directions for students:

Step 1   **OBSERVE:** Look carefully at the slide presented for the prescribed amount of time.

Step 2   **READ:** Read any writing on the slide.

Step 3   **THINK:** Think about what the slide is showing. Make connections, ask questions, and react with your emotions.

Step 4   **DISCUSS:** Talk with your group about what you see.

Step 5   **WRITE:** Respond to each slide in the appropriate spot on the handout, "Slide Show Preview." Responses can include an opinion, a connection, a question, an idea, or an emotion.

Step 6   **SHARE:** (Optional) Share your responses with your group.

Example: Prior to reading the book *To Be a Slave* (Lester 1968), students were shown a PowerPoint® collection of images related to the concepts of slavery and freedom. Slides included statistics, quotations, photographs, artist renderings, maps, and a short video clip of an interview. There were 10 slides in all. Here is a sampling of different students' responses to one of these slides—a quote by Abraham Lincoln:

"Whenever I hear someone arguing for slavery,

I feel a strong impulse to see it tried on him personally."

Student responses:

- *That's kinda like treating others the way you want to be treated.*

- *I would hate to be treated like a slave!*

- *Lincoln seems like a caring person.*

- *What possible argument could someone make for slavery?*

- *After the Civil War, maybe everyone who had a slave should have **been** one for a week or something.*

- *I wonder how long one of the persons arguing for slavery would actually be a slave before his or her mind would change completely.*

- *It seems that this statement came straight from Lincoln's gut. It's a pretty strong statement!*

Slide Show Preview

Student Handout

Write a response to each slide. Responses can include your opinion, a personal connection, a reaction, a question, or an idea it brings to mind.

Slide #	Response
1	
2	
3	
4	
5	
6	

Name _____ Date _____

MAKING CONNECTIONS

Type of text: Literature or informational text

Standards addressed: Standards related to: connecting a text to previously learned concepts; asking questions to acquire information; integrating and evaluating information in a variety of formats; producing clear and coherent writing; effectively engaging in collaborations and discussions; vocabulary acquisition and use; conventions of standard English; and knowledge and use of language.

CCSS: ELA-Literacy. RL.6-8.7, 10; RI.6-8.7, 10; RH.6-8.7, 10; RST.6-8.7, 10; W.6-8.4, 6, 7, 10; WHST.6-8.4, 6, 7, 10; SL.6-8.1-2, 4, 6; L.6-8.1-6

Approximate time: One class period

Materials and preparation: Copies of student handout "Making Connections" (prepared by teacher, based on the reading task and using the template on page 58)

Overview: This pre-reading lesson requires students to think about their own background knowledge and connect it to several facets of the text they're going to read.

Information for teachers: The students are asked to recall their own knowledge on a specific subject as a foundation for future learning that will come from engagement with a text or texts on the subject. You'll guide them in this task with a handout that gives words and phrases related to the subject. Use the student handout template, "Making Connections with...," on page 58. The handout can be readily adapted to fit any reading task.

Technology connections: In many cases, online biographical articles will have links to supplemental information, pictures, timelines, quotations, and other details about a historical figure, a scientific topic, or the idea, setting, or theme of a fictional work. Also, students can share questions in online formats or with digital devices.

Arts connections: Students can try to communicate one of the connections they noticed or one of their questions without using words (e.g., through mime, dance, or other movement, drawing, or painting).

Strategies for differentiation: As this lesson draws on students' previous knowledge only, it is already differentiated. Some students may need help with pronunciations of the words; others may need prompts or examples to get them started.

Assessment: As this is a pre-reading assignment, assessment should be based on completion of the handout and discussion of student responses only. It is more important to validate students' individual connections and experiences rather than to evaluate them.

Directions for students:

Step 1   **READ:** Read the key words or phrases on the handout your teacher prepared.

Step 2   **RESPOND:** Put a checkmark in the column that best fits your connection to each idea or item listed.

Step 3   **ASK:** At the end, write three questions you're wondering about the assigned text before you do the actual reading.

Step 4   **DISCUSS:** With a small group of classmates, share and discuss your connections and questions.

Example: In this classroom, students were studying influential scientists. They were asked to read autobiographical and biographical articles. Here is an example of the pre-reading preparation by one student before he read about Sir Isaac Newton:

Making Connections with

Sir Isaac Newton

(topic of text I will read)

Put a check in the box that best describes the connection you make with the word or phrase below. You can check more than one box for each word or phrase.

Student Handout

Word or Phrase Related to the Text to Be Read	I've never heard of this.	I can make a connection with something I've experienced.	I can make a connection with something I've read.	I can make a connection with other knowledge that I have (from movies, TV, etc.).
Isaac Newton			✓	
astronomer			✓	
being more interested in building things than in studying		✓		✓
mathematics		✓		
physics			✓	
making discoveries		✓	✓	✓
gravity		✓	✓	✓
calculus	✓			
optics		✓	✓	
telescope		✓	✓	✓
Cambridge University				✓
Westminster Abbey	✓			

Here are three questions I have about some of the above information.

1. What does Newton have to do with optics?

2. Was Newton maybe someone who wanted to build things instead of studying—like me?

3. Did Newton invent the telescope?

Name _____ Date _____

Making Connections with

_____

(topic of text I will read)

Put a check in the box that best describes the connection you make with the word or phrase below. You can check more than one box for each word or phrase.

Student Handout

Word or Phrase Related to the Text to Be Read	I've never heard of this.	I can make a connection with something I've experienced.	I can make a connection with something I've read.	I can make a connection with other knowledge that I have (from movies, TV, etc.).

Here are three questions I have about some of the above information.

1.

2.

3.

Name _____ Date _____

GROUP PRE-READING: WHAT? AND WHY?

Type of text: Literature or informational text

Standards addressed: Standards related to: skimming a text; close examination of key ideas and details; drawing inferences and conclusions; asking questions to learn about texts; examining text structure to see how it contributes to meaning and message; integrating and evaluating information in a variety of formats; identifying author's purpose; determining meaning of words and phrases as they are used in a text; acquiring and using vocabulary; writing explanatory text; producing clear and coherent writing; effectively engaging in collaborations and discussions; conventions of standard English; and knowledge and use of language.

CCSS: ELA-Literacy. RL.6-8.1-7, 10; RI.6-8.1-7, 10; RH.6-8.1-7, 10; RST.6-8.1-7, 10; W.6-8.2, 4, 6-7, 9-10; WHST.6-8.2, 4, 6-7, 9-10; SL.6-8.1-2; L.6-8.1-6

Approximate time: 10 to 30 minutes depending on the complexity of the reading task

Materials and preparation: Text; copies of student handout "What? And Why? Group Discussion Guide" (page 62)

Overview: This lesson helps students "put their heads together" to anticipate the structure of a text as well as to determine a purpose for reading. The work can be recorded on a sheet of paper, on an online sharing site, or on a poster for visual impact.

Information for teachers: This lesson can be done in such a way that the whole class is preparing to read the same text (such as a science textbook chapter or an article), or it can work in the same way if small groups of students are preparing to read different texts (e.g., book groups). Form students into small groups of three or four students. Each group will need one facilitator to keep the students on task and one recorder to write down each group member's ideas.

Lessons Before Reading

10

Group Pre-Reading: What? And Why?, page 2

Technology connections: This discussion also works well as a shared online document or on an online bulletin board/posting site such as Glogster® or Padlet™.

Arts connections: Students might take on the challenge of creating a visual representation to answer the questions "What?" (What is the structure?) and "Why?" (In your opinion, why did the writer choose the structure?).

Strategies for differentiation: Groups should be differentiated based on what they're reading. Groups may be heterogeneous or homogeneous depending on the texts and the needs of the specific class.

Assessment: This lesson is best assessed on completion only because it is based on previewing only and not on specific reading skills. Observe student participation in and contributions to the group process and responses on the discussion guide.

What? Why?

Directions for students:

Step 1 **DECIDE:** In your group, decide who will facilitate (keep everyone on task) and who will record (write down what you learn).

Step 2 **PREVIEW:** Scan the text you will be reading.

Step 3 **DISCUSS:** Talk about the questions on the "What? and Why?" group discussion guide. Be sure that everyone gets a chance to be heard.

Step 4 **RECORD:** Have your recorder write down a summary of the group's discussion. Or, everyone in the group can record responses individually on a shared online document or a large poster.

Group Pre-Reading: What? And Why?, page 3

Lessons Before
Reading
10

Example:

Here are some sample student responses to the questions "What? and Why?" from the group discussion guide (see page 62). These responses were taken from assignments related to different texts—fiction and informational.

Fiction

- *The text is divided into sections with date labels. Within the sections, it is divided into short chapters. Each chapter is labeled with a character's name and a date. The dates show that the story is not in chronological order. (Question 3)*

- *The author may be trying to tell the story from the viewpoints of several different characters. She might be jumping back and forth in dates to keep the reader interested and guessing and not knowing the whole story until the end. (Question 4)*

- *There is a map at the beginning of each story. Readers might need to refer to the maps to understand some of the events in the story. (Questions 3 and 4)*

- *The intended audience seems to be teenagers or pre-teenagers. (Question 5)*

- *The book has a catchy title and we've liked other books by this author. (Question 6)*

Nonfiction

- *The article has sections on different kinds of space phenomena. Each section has many subsections on specific topics. There are lots of subtitles, bold words, diagrams, pictures, and sketches. There is a lot of information in the captions. (Question 3)*

- *It looks like the structure of this would help to give information in short bits to help the reader really understand about the different items. (Question 4)*

- *We think the intended audience is anybody who is a fairly good reader and who is interested in amazing space stuff. (Question 5)*

- *We would read this article to find out about black holes, white holes, Jupiter's red spots, dark matter, meteor storms, and other interesting things in space. (Questions 6 and 7)*

What? And Why? Group Discussion Guide

Text _____ Date _____

Group members _____

(Your recorder should write notes as you discuss these questions.
There may be several answers for some of the questions.)

Student Handout

1. What is the title of the text we're going to read?

2. How long is the text? _____ What genre (kind) of text is it?

3. What is the general structure of the text? (How is it divided? Are there sections? Chapters?) What is included with the text (e.g., titles, subtitles, or illustrations)?

4. Why might a writer choose to use this structure?

5. Who is the intended audience for this text?

6. Why read this text? (What are the main purposes for reading it?)

7. What are some things group members hope to learn from reading this text?

Name _____ Date _____

PART 2
LESSONS
DURING
READING

Reading should not be presented to
children as a chore or duty.
It should be offered to them
as a precious gift.

~Kate DiCamillo

Contents

The term "Lessons During Reading" does not mean that students are reading and doing something else simultaneously. Rather "during," in this context, means that these lessons work well somewhere between the beginning of reading a text and the end.

These tasks are meant to enhance students' understanding as they work through a text, helping them master a text section by section. This means that the tasks work best with small pieces of text rather than whole articles, books, dramas, or essays.

Many of these lessons could easily be repeated throughout a unit. For example, students could write a summary (pages 65-69) and participate in questioning (pages 80-83) after every section of a lengthy article or chapter of a book.

Beyond increasing comprehension, many of these lessons are also designed to improve cooperation, presentation skills, and motivation. Students who engage with text in a variety of ways will likely be better and more enthusiastic readers.

EYE-CATCHING SUMMARIES

Type of text: Literature or informational text

Standards addressed: Standards related to: skimming a text; determining the central ideas and supporting details of a text; analyzing development of ideas, characters, and events over the course of a text; summarizing a text; analyzing and presenting main ideas in a variety of formats; determining meanings of words and phrases as they are used in a text; writing informational or narrative text; producing clear and coherent writing; revising writing; effectively engaging in collaborations and discussions; and presenting knowledge and ideas using a variety of components—including the arts and technology; conventions of standard English; and knowledge and use of language.

CCSS: ELA-Literacy.RL.6-8.1-4, 7, 10; RI.6-8.1-4, 7, 10; RH.6-8.1-4, 7, 10; RST.6-8.1-4, 10; W.6-8.2-6, 9-10; WHST.6-8. 6-8.2, 4-6, 9-10; SL.6-8.1-2, 4-6; L.6-8.1-6

Approximate lesson time: 20 minutes per summary

Materials and preparation: Text (choose a short text or short section of a longer text); copies of student handout (teacher-prepared handout following the models on pages 68-69, adapted to include the name of the text, number of words for the summary, and number of lines for the summary)

Overview: This lesson helps students identify key words in a text, find words that contribute to the same theme, and write succinct and accurate summaries.

Information for teachers: There are dozens (if not hundreds) of ways to encourage students to write good summaries. This lesson works well for students of all ages as it adds a visual component to summarizing—students can picture exactly what a 10-word summary (or any other number of words) looks like before they begin. The visual component is strengthened when the lines or spaces for the words are formed into a visual aid (such as a shape or picture). Alternatively, students can form their summaries into a picture when they're finished with the summaries.

Information for teachers, continued:

Students read a selection and then write a summary using only the number of words prescribed (pre-selected by the teacher). You might allow students to start with longer summaries then work through a summary a few times, slowly cutting the number of words down to help them get to just the key words.

After writing summaries, students compare and discuss them to check for effective use of the word allotment. Students can also trade and compare summaries. Then students revise their own work using ideas gathered from a partner or group.

If desired, the lesson could include a competition where students give point ratings to score summaries according to criteria of giving an accurate summary; surprising or otherwise engaging the audience; and making good use of the limited number of words.

Technology connections: Use online passages or online documents as the base text for summaries. The activity can also be loaded into an online reading program that enables highlighting (e.g., diigo.com and scrible.com) or students can use such an app as GoodNotes® or Evernote®. Also, an activity that leads to short summaries (10, 15, 20 or so words) cries out for tweeting! Where students have the capability and school rules allow, students can share their summaries with a tweet or a text.

Arts connections: Instead of using a prepared visual form for writing their summaries, students might design their own artistic arrangements for summaries, connecting the artistic design to the topic or theme of the text. For example, to summarize Robert Frost's poem, "Fire and Ice," a student might form words for 16 lines into a shape or design that suggests a flame or a block of ice. (See page 69.)

Strategies for differentiation: This lesson works for students of all levels, assuming the reading selection itself is appropriate. For students who have difficulty reading the selected content, it's best to start with shorter passages.

Assessment: As students compare, discuss, and revise their summaries, a good deal of self-assessment will take place. In this discussion process, encourage them to look for good use of the limited words. They might ask, "Whose summary gives complete information about the piece in the limited space provided?" If needed, you might give students points for following directions and for using the correct number of words.

Directions for students:

Step 1   **READ:** Skim the reading passage provided by the teacher. Look for key ideas and words that communicate key ideas or the main theme of the text.

Step 2   **THINK and PLAN:** Think about how you can use a limited number of well-chosen words to summarize the key point, plot, or theme of the text.

Step 3   **WRITE:** Using the number of words specified in the assignment, summarize the text. Refer to the handout your teacher gave you showing models of summaries.

Step 4   **DISCUSS:** Share and discuss the summaries in small groups or as a whole class. Look for effective use of the limited number of words. Give feedback to each writer.

Step 5   **REWRITE:** Rewrite your summary based on feedback from your peers and ideas you got from sharing work with each other. Reduce the number of words in your summary, if needed, to fulfill the assignment.

Eye-Catching Summaries, page 4

Example: Students were directed to read the following paragraph and summarize the information using **exactly** 14 words.

Cleopatra, *«klee uh PAT ruh»* (69-30 B.C.), was a queen of ancient Egypt and one of the most fascinating women in history. Through the years, she gained a reputation for beauty, but scholars disagree about her appearance. They agree, however, that she was intelligent, charming, witty, and ambitious. At times, Cleopatra was ruthless. However, she took a great interest in her subjects' welfare and won their affection. She developed romantic

relationships with Julius Caesar and Mark Antony, two of the greatest Roman leaders of her day.

Cleopatra belonged to the *dynasty* (series of rulers in the same family) founded by Ptolemy I in 323 B.C. Ptolemy was a general in the army of the Macedonian conqueror Alexander the Great. Cleopatra is also known as Cleopatra VII because she was the seventh Egyptian queen of Macedonian descent with that name.

Source: Ritner, Robert K. "Cleopatra." *World Book Student.* World Book, 2014. Web. 20 Jan. 2016.

Here are two sample summaries:

Queen

of   ancient   Egypt,

fascinating,   intelligent,   ruthless,

loved   Caesar   and   Mark   Antony,   army general

Cleopatra	was	queen	of	ancient	Egypt,
maybe	beautiful,	definitely	a	leader,	had
two	boyfriends				

Eye-Catching Summaries, page 5

Example: Here's a sample of a student assignment that a teacher prepared for a specific text. A seventh-grade student created the summary.

Eye-Catching Summary

Read the text of the poem. Then summarize the poem, using **exactly** 16 words.

Fire and Ice

by Robert Frost

Some say the world will end in fire,
Some say in ice.
From what I've tasted of desire
I hold with those who favor fire.
But if it had to perish twice,
I think I know enough of hate
To say that for destruction ice
Is also great
And would suffice.

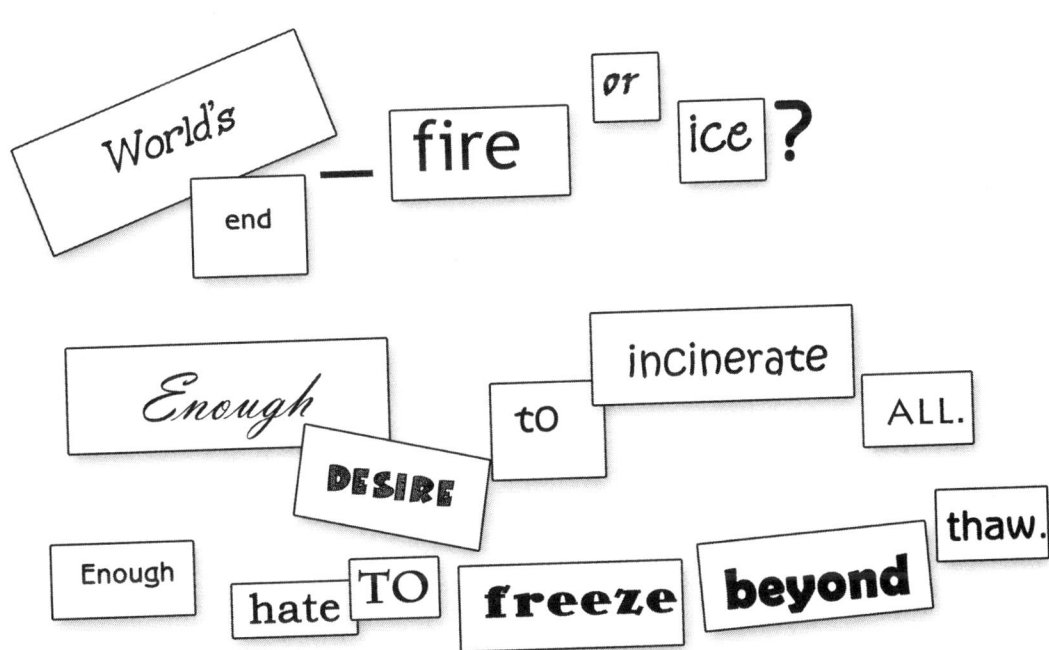

EXPLORE THE SETTING

Type of text: Historical fiction, realistic fiction (stories that could actually have occurred in a believable setting), or nonfiction (including biography and informational text—as long as it is a text with an identifiable setting)

Standards addressed: Standards related to: close reading of key ideas and details in a text; drawing inferences and conclusions; analyzing particular elements of a story or informational text; summarizing or paraphrasing; identifying setting and analyzing its role in a text; integrating elements of a story or informational text; researching to build knowledge; gathering and presenting relevant information from multiple digital sources; writing explanatory, informational, or narrative text; producing clear and coherent writing; effectively engaging in collaborations and discussions; conventions of standard English; and knowledge and use of language.

CCSS: ELA-Literacy.RL.6-8.1-3, 5, 7, 10; RI.6-8.1-3, 5, 7, 10; RH.6-8.1-2, 5, 7, 10; RST.6-8.1-2, 5, 7, 10; W.6-8.2-4, 6-10; WHST.6-8.2-4, 6-10; SL.6-8.1-2, 4-6; L.6-8.1-3, 6

Approximate lesson time: 30 to 40 minutes

Materials and preparation: Text; copies of student handout "Explore the Setting" (page 74); computers with Internet access (minimum one per group)

Overview: This lesson gives students visual reference points for the setting of the text they're reading, helping to connect the setting to the plot and main ideas, to real geographic locations, and to other information the student finds through research. Students develop a sense of the importance of the setting in furthering the message or story of the text.

Information for teachers: Begin this lesson at any point in the reading when students have enough information about the setting to begin their research. If access to technology is limited, students can share computers and work in groups. Some discussion time will allow them to collaborate on their findings, and will inspire them to pay even closer attention to the settings as they continue to read. As they read more of the text, they can repeat the activity—adding more of what they learn about the setting and the part it plays in the meaning or impact of the text.

Technology connections: In addition to using the Internet for research, students can take "virtual tours" of places related to the text. They might also present their findings using such technology as PowerPoint®, Keynote®, or Google Slides™.

Arts connections: It is natural for a reader to visualize settings from a text; encourage readers to take time to do this! Suggest that students add their own sketches, diagrams, simple maps, or other visuals that communicate something about the setting.

Strategies for differentiation: If a narrower search is desired, the teacher can provide two or three specific sites and direct students to those. Possibilities include online encyclopedias, museum websites, or relevant online videos. The teacher can also design more specific questions ahead of time or simply allow the students to see what they can find on these sites and use the handout template on page 74 as it is. Students less familiar with technology could be paired with classroom "experts."

Assessment: Assess work recorded on the handout, focusing on students' abilities to find and record the setting(s) accurately, use reliable and appropriate resources, and summarize what they've learned.

Directions for students:

Step 1   **READ:** Read the assigned pages, paying close attention to all aspects of the setting. Notice if there is more than one setting in the text.

Step 2   **CONNECT:** Also as you read, look for ways that the setting(s) is connected to the development of the plot or key ideas of the text. Ask yourself, "How does the setting(s) make a difference?"

Step 3   **RECALL and WRITE:** As you recall one or two settings throughout the text, record them on the handout, "Explore the Setting."

Step 4   **RESEARCH:** Use the Internet or other classroom resources to conduct research about the setting(s). Look for articles, maps, videos, and anything else that gives information about the setting(s).

Step 5   **SUMMARIZE:** Summarize and paraphrase your research on the handout. Use more paper, if needed.

Step 6   **DISCUSS:** In your group, discuss this question: "From what you can tell from the text so far, how is the setting(s) critical to the development of the story (literature) or key ideas (informational text)?"

Step 7   **READ:** As you continue to read, your research can help you to explore and understand the setting(s) more deeply. Continue to notice how the author develops the setting(s) and how the setting(s) contribute to the text as a whole.

Explore the Setting, page 4

Example:  Students completed this lesson as they read the novel, *The Fault in Our Stars*, by John Green (2013).

- They identified these settings of the story: Indianapolis, Amsterdam, a hospital, and the church basement where a cancer support group meets.

- Groups were responsible for finding images online, citing their sources, and sharing the images with the class. Some groups of students used Internet map sites to locate and find pictures of Amsterdam and Indianapolis. Other groups researched cancer support groups and the emotional aspects of having cancer. Some skimmed articles about Amsterdam or cancer hospitals.

- Under what they learned, students reported such ideas as attractions and culture of Amsterdam; differences between the location, weather, and cultures of Indianapolis and Amsterdam; and how close and important the people in a cancer support group become to one another.

- A group of students noticed the role that one of the settings in the book played in the plot development. They said: "The setting of Amsterdam pulls Gus and Hazel into a life that is opposite from their lives in the hospital and the routine of living under the shadow of cancer. It gives them adventure and freedom and romance—things they have not experienced in their routines of dealing with their cancer."

Explore the Setting

Text title and author _____

Student Handout

A. As you read, identify the settings of the story or informational text. Choose one or two settings and record any aspects of setting that you notice. Remember to look for physical setting (such as place, weather, surroundings), time (such as date, era, season, time of day), and social situation (including customs, politics, morals).

Physical Setting	Time	Social Situation

B. Now use your Internet search skills to research one item from each category and see what you can discover. Record your work below.

Sources I used:

Things I learned:

From what you can tell from the text so far, give one idea about how the setting(s) is critical to the story or key ideas:

Note: You will also be asked to show and/or print one image you found while researching.

Name _____ Date _____

CHARACTER DIARY RETELLINGS

Type of text: Narrative text that includes a character (real or fictitious)

Standards addressed: Standards related to: close reading of key ideas and details in a text; determining theme or central ideas; drawing inferences and conclusions; analyzing particular elements of a story or informational text; determining point of view; character development and analysis; retelling; identifying purpose; integrating elements of a story; writing narrative text; producing clear and coherent writing; revising writing; conventions of standard English; and knowledge and use of language.

CCSS: ELA-Literacy.RL.6-8.1-3, 6-7, 10; RI.6-8.1-3, 6-7, 10; RH.6-8.1-3, 6-7, 10; RST.6-8.1-3, 6-7, 10; W.6-8.3-10; WHST.6-8.3-10; SL.2-6; L.6-8.1-3, 6

Approximate lesson time: 30 to 40 minutes plus time another day for dramatic readings (Step 6 in Directions for students on page 77) and for evaluations

Materials and preparation: Text; copies of teacher-prepared diary assignment on a student handout (see sample on page 78); copies of scoring rubric "Character Diary Rubric" (page 79) or a similar rubric you create

Overview: This lesson helps students examine and get to know a character in a text, understand and take on the character's voice and point of view, and check the students' comprehension of the reading. In addition, the students practice their narrative writing skills and revise and polish a written passage. Finally, they give a dramatic reading of their original diary entry to showcase their selected character.

Information for teachers: Plan to use this lesson after any important event in a text (such as a challenge, a loss, a celebration, or an "ah-ha moment"). The task is to have students retell an event, writing in diary form (first person), from a different perspective than what is given. For example, if a story is told from the main character's point of view, have the students write a diary entry from another character's point of view. If a story is told in third person, have the students write the entry in first person to "get inside the character's head." The sample assignment here (page 78) is for one specific text (*A Christmas Carol*), but can be adapted readily to any other.

Before students begin Step 3 of their process (the writing), discuss with them the components of a good diary entry (including the date, speaking with authentic voice, using first person, and using sensory language to help the audience picture what happened). Also provide students with a copy of the rubric (page 79) and discuss it with them.

Technology connections: This assignment can easily be done on a computer and shared electronically. It can also be read and recorded as a video diary or shared on a podcast. Students can record themselves reading the diary entry, using a site like Vocaroo.com. Or they can video themselves on a tablet or smartphone.

Strategies for differentiation: Students who have difficulty with such a reading task can be given a graphic organizer beforehand to help them list the important events in Scrooge's day before they retell them. Advanced students should be encouraged to imitate Scrooge's British idiom and accent as they write and as they read aloud.

Assessment: This writing task can be assessed as an in-class essay or a multistep writing assignment with revisions and a polished final version. A standards-based rubric is included. The traits to be evaluated are readily adaptable to assessing writing standards from any set of college- and career-ready standards. This rubric allows for teacher, student, and peer assessment.

Directions for students:

Step 1   **READ:** Read the assigned text pages, paying close attention to the traits of the characters.

Step 2   **THINK:** Imagine that you are _____ (specific character and time) and think about what it's like to be in your situation. What are your thoughts? Emotions? Challenges? Ideas? Decisions to be made? Dilemmas?

Step 3   **WRITE:** Follow the directions on your diary entry assignment for writing a diary entry to write a one-page diary entry from the point of view of your character. Stay true to your character's voice and personality. Review the student handout "Character Diary Rubric" before you write. This will help you identify the characteristics of a well-written narrative.

Step 4   **EDIT and REVISE:** Use the rubric to guide you.

Step 5   **DRAMATIZE:** Give a dramatic reading of your diary entry to a small group of classmates.

Step 6   **EVALUATE:** Use the "Character Diary Rubric" to evaluate your own diary presentation and presentations of your classmates.

Example: After reading the first section (called "Stave 1") of *A Christmas Carol*,
 by Charles Dickens (1843), students were given an assignment to write
a diary entry from the point of view of the main character, Ebenezer
Scrooge. In the story, told in third person, Scrooge is exhausted and goes
straight to bed at the end of a long day. In this assignment, students
were asked to imagine that Scrooge stayed up and wrote about his day,
staying true to his voice and personality. Before students began the
assignment, the class talked about Scrooge's frame of mind and mood at
that point in the story and brainstormed some of the kinds of things he
might write in his diary.

Scrooge's Diary Assignment
(End of Stave 1)

Imagine that Scrooge sat down to write in his
diary on December 24th, 1843, instead of going
straight to bed. Based on what you know about
Scrooge's personality so far, write Scrooge's diary
entry.

In two to three paragraphs, express his thoughts
and feelings about his day and his encounter with
Marley's ghost. Be as specific as you can, including
details from the story. Use first-person point
of view. (In other words, write as if you ARE
Scrooge.)

Use the "Character Diary Rubric"
to guide your writing.

Character Diary Rubric

Scoring Guide:

4 = **Advanced** = exceeds all criteria

3 = **Proficient** = meets 80 to 100% of criteria

2 = **Partially Proficient** = meets some (60 to 79%) of criteria

1 = **Unsatisfactory** = meets less than 60% of criteria

Trait	Description	Self Score	Peer Score	Teacher Score
Ideas	Uses narrative techniques, such as dialogue, pacing, description, and reflection, to develop experiences, events, and/or characters. Accurately retells portions of the story from a fresh perspective.			
Organization	Engages and orients the reader by establishing a context and point of view and introducing a narrator and/or characters; organizes an event sequence that unfolds naturally and logically. Provides a conclusion that follows from and reflects on the narrated experiences or events.			
Fluency	Uses a variety of transition words, phrases, and clauses to convey sequence, signal shifts from one time frame or setting to another, and show the relationships among experiences and events.			
Word Choice	Uses precise words and phrases, relevant descriptive details, and sensory language to capture the action and convey experiences and events.			
Voice	Accurately reflects the chosen character's personality and experiences.			
Conventions	Demonstrates command of the conventions of standard English capitalization, punctuation, and spelling when writing.			

Name _____ Date _____

THE QUESTIONING HABIT

Type of text: Literature or informational text

Standards addressed: Standards related to: close reading of key ideas and details in a text; drawing inferences; identifying key concepts within the text; asking questions about a text; finding answers and information within a text; getting to deeper meanings in a text; examining meanings of words and phrases in a text; producing clear and coherent writing; effectively engaging in collaborations and discussions; conventions of standard English; and knowledge and use of language.

CCSS: ELA-Literacy.RL.6-8.1-8, 10; RI.6-8.1-8, 10; RH.6-8.1-8, 10; RST.6-8.1-8, 10; W.6-8.4, 6, 9-10; WHST.6-8.4, 6, 9-10; SL.6-8.1-2, 6; L.6-8.1-4, 6

Approximate lesson time: 5 to 20 minutes (or more)

Materials and preparation: Text; sticky notes for students

Overview: Good readers ask and answer questions as they read. This lesson is designed to help students develop this habit.

Information for teachers: Assign a text or portion of a text, depending on the length of the whole. If a text is long, break the text into "chunks" and repeat this activity after students read each portion. Students can do this activity individually, in groups, or as a class. It is best if they can see each other's questions to prompt discussion and avoid too much repetition.

When you direct students for this questioning lesson, encourage collaboration. Assure them that all kinds of questions are acceptable. Part of the goal here is to develop the habit of asking questions, rather than to elicit specific types.

As an extension to this assignment, you might require your students to write one of each type of question mentioned in Step 2 of the student directions.

Technology connections: Students can use online resources to research questions that are unanswered at the end of the lesson unit. This lesson also works well when students post their questions on an electronic bulletin board or forum or share questions on a platform such as Schoology® or Google Classroom™.

Strategies for differentiation: The lesson allows for differentiation in its very nature; students will ask questions at their own level of understanding.

Assessment: Assess students on number and quality of questions. For example, you could award a point for any appropriate question that ties to the text.

Directions for students:

Step 1   **READ:** Read the assigned text.

Step 2   **ASK QUESTIONS:** They might be questions that are answered in the text, or questions that can be researched, or questions that don't have an obvious answer. All types are acceptable.

Step 3   **WRITE:** Write your most pressing question or what you think is your best question on a sticky note.

Step 4   **POST:** Post the question on the board. If you see that someone else has the same question, put your sticky note on top of his or hers.

Step 5   **THINK:** Think about the questions that everyone has asked and reflect on how the questions add layers of understanding to the text.

Step 6   **REVISIT:** Come back to the questions when the whole text is read or at the end of the unit. Talk with classmates about which questions were answered, which need further research, and how you might find answers to unanswered questions.

The Questioning Habit, page 3

Example (fictional text): Here's a paragraph from Jude Watson's *Loot* (Scholastic, 2014, p. 1) along with a few questions that students posted about the text.

No thief likes a full moon. Like mushrooms and owls, they do their best work in the dark. There it is, a fat, satisfied moon, bright and silvery white, tracing a line on the dark lake that leads right to three thieves, who have paused to examine the loot. It has been the perfect heist. In and out, a hot knife through sweet butter. Months of planning, practice runs, disagreements that ballooned into fights.

How is the moon fat?

What did they steal?

What had made the heist "perfect"?

What kind of loot do the thieves have?

More Examples:
- *What were the disagreements?*
- *What did the thieves fight about?*
- *Were the thieves friends?*
- *What would make a moon "satisfied"?*
- *Why do some people steal things that aren't theirs?*

Will they get away with it?

Do mushrooms really grow in the dark?

What does "heist" mean?

The Questioning Habit, page 4

Example (informational text): Here's a selection from an encyclopedia article, along with a few questions that students posted about the text.

Cricket is a jumping insect related to grasshoppers. The wings of most crickets lie flat over each other on top of their backs. Other crickets have only tiny wings or are wingless. The slender *antennae* (feelers) grow much longer than the body in most kinds of crickets. Female crickets lay eggs through a long, needlelike *ovipositor*.

How a cricket "sings"
The songs of crickets are produced mainly by the males. Each kind of cricket has a different song, usually trills or a series of chirps. Crickets make sound by rubbing their two front wings together. They hear sound with organs in their front legs. The songs help males and females find each other. Crickets commonly live in pastures and meadows and along roads. Sometimes they enter houses. Crickets eat plants and the remains of other insects.

The best-known crickets include the *house cricket* of Europe and the *common, black,* or *field cricket* of the United States. These black or brown insects measure about 1 inch (2.5 centimeters) long. *Tree crickets* are white or pale green. They live on trees and shrubs and feed on small insects called *aphids.* Male tree crickets sing in chorus. Their song is a high-pitched *treet-treet-treet.* The tiny *ant-loving crickets* are wingless and as broad as they are long. They live in ants' nests and eat ants' young. *Mormon crickets, camel (cave) crickets, mole crickets,* and *Jerusalem crickets* are not considered true crickets.

Faber, Betty Lane. "Cricket." *World Book Student*. World Book, 2014. Web. 20 Jan. 2016.

How can a cricket be wingless?

Do crickets without wings still make noise?

Where do crickets lay their eggs?

Why do the males sing more than the females?

Do some people eat crickets?

JIGSAW

Type of text: Informational text

Standards addressed: Standards related to: skimming a text; determining the central idea of a text; providing a clear summary of a text; identifying key concepts within the text; analyzing and presenting main ideas in a variety of formats; determining meaning of words and phrases as they are used in a text; writing explanatory or informational text; producing clear and coherent writing; revising writing; actively listening; effectively engaging in collaborations and discussions; and presenting knowledge and ideas using a variety of components— including the arts and technology; conventions of standard English; and knowledge and use of language.

CCSS: ELA-Literacy.RI.6-8.1-5, 7-8, 10; RH.6-8.1-5, 7-8, 10; RST.6-8.1-5, 7-8, 10; W.6-8.2, 4-5, 9-10; WHST.6-8.2, 4-5, 9-10; SL.6-8.1-2, 4-6; L.6-8.1-4, 6

Approximate time: One class period (or longer depending on the length of the selections)

Materials and preparation: Text; division of students into groups of 4–5 (best if all groups are the same size); puzzle pieces for each student or group

Overview: This lesson will help students learn a variety of information in a limited amount of time. The overall topic or selection to be read is a "puzzle," and each student is responsible for a piece. When put together, the picture is clarified for students because they see the whole.

Information for teachers: A key to this lesson is the division of the text to be read into sections. There are several ways to divide the material. Two basic ways are (1) give each member of a small group one piece of the "puzzle" (text) to read and share in their own group; and (2) give each *group* one piece of the "puzzle" to read and have the groups share out to the whole class.

Information for teachers, continued:

Begin with a large piece of poster board. Cut it into jigsaw-style puzzle pieces. Give a piece to each student (if using option 1 above) or to each group (if using option 2 above). Students will use the puzzle pieces for their summaries. As they share, they can physically put the puzzle together. (Blank cardboard puzzle pieces can be purchased online or at craft stores.) If puzzle pieces are laminated, students can work with dry erase markers so that the pieces can be reused.

Technology connections: Give students the challenge of finding ways to share their puzzle-making process or completed puzzles electronically or through multimedia presentations.

Strategies for differentiation: Form groups that pair struggling readers with proficient readers. The teacher can also decide ahead of time which group reads which section of the text (based on students' abilities).

Assessment: After the jigsaw puzzle is complete, have each group write one or two quiz questions; those can be compiled and used to assess the lesson.

Directions for students:

Step 1 **READ:** Read your assigned section of the text carefully, focusing on developments or important facts and concepts.

Step 2 **THINK:** Think about what you read and how you would summarize it in a way that can be shared with others.

Step 3 **SUMMARIZE:** On your puzzle piece, write, draw, or diagram something that summarizes the important developments, concepts, or facts in your text.

Step 4 **LISTEN, SHOW, and SHARE:** Listen to others share their summarizing pieces of the puzzle by telling, demonstrating, drawing, or dramatizing. Then share yours. Together you will all form the "big picture."

Jigsaw, page 3

Example: As an introduction to physical science, students explored an article on physics.

(http://worldbookonline.com/student/article?id=ar428580&st=physics)

- The class was divided into 10 groups of three students each. The teacher assigned one of these sections from the article to each group:

   Mechanics

   Heat

   Sound

   Electricity and magnetism

   Light

   Atomic, molecular, and electron physics

   Nuclear physics

   Particle physics

   Solid-state physics

   Fluid and plasma physics

- Each group member had one of these roles: facilitator, recorder, or reporter.

- Each group read its own section and discussed it. The facilitator made sure that everyone's voice was heard and that the text was covered completely. The recorder took notes. Group members discussed and agreed on the content and format with which they would create the puzzle piece.

- Finally, groups assembled the jigsaw, and the reporter from each group shared the information from his or her group's piece with the class.

READ-ALOUD BROADCASTS

Type of text: Literature or informational text

Standards addressed: Standards related to: engaging with a text; identifying and describing author's voice; listening comprehension; presenting knowledge and ideas using a variety of components—including the arts and technology; adapting speech to a variety of contexts and tasks; conventions of standard English; and knowledge and use of language.

CCSS: ELA-Literacy.SL.6-8.1-2, 4-6; L.6-8.1-4, 6

Approximate time: 40 minutes (varies depending on selection)

Materials and preparation: Texts to be read; recording equipment (microphones, tablets, computers, digital voice recorders, etc.); copies of student handout, "Read-Aloud Feedback" (page 89)

Overview: This lesson brings a text to life and puts the students' voices into the material. It gives students a way to express excitement about a text and to share it with others.

Information for teachers: This works best when students have had time to practice aloud, either with a partner or into a microphone. Recording their voices increases motivation and improves fluency. See that their recordings find an audience or multiple audiences. There are numerous apps and websites available for sharing recordings. (Try one of Google's® free apps, Smart Voice Recorder or VoiceThread™, or a free Apple app for the iPad called Voice Record Pro. Or students can use one of these websites: vocaroo.com or voicethread.com.)

Arts connections: Students can add background music and sound effects to their recordings.

Strategies for differentiation: This lesson can also be done in pairs or small groups, with different students reading different parts by alternating paragraphs. Differentiation can also occur through the selection of the texts to be read.

Assessment: Students give evaluative feedback to one another by completing the handout "Read-Aloud Feedback" (page 89). This can also be used as a self-evaluative tool.

Directions for students:

Step 1   **READ ALOUD:** Practice reading your text. Use vocal clarity and inflection to bring the text to life.

Step 2   **RECORD:** Record your text! Do it in one "take" if you can.

Step 3   **LISTEN:** Listen and check out how you sound. Follow along on the page as you listen and check yourself for accuracy.

Step 4   **SHARE:** Let others listen to your recording. This can be done online or in person depending on the technology used.

Step 5   **EVALUATE:** Use the student handout "Read-Aloud Feedback" to give feedback to each other on the read-aloud recordings.

Examples: Students can:

- create and record readers' theater with a variety of stories or dramas.
- record stories, myths, anecdotes, or poems for listening experiences for younger students.
- read articles, adapting information on interesting topics to present to classmates or younger students.
- record themselves reading poetry or children's books with a variety of voices.

Read-Aloud Feedback

Name of reader _____

Title of text _____

Name of evaluator_____Date _____

Circle the score that applies for each component of the read-aloud performance.

Student Handout

1. Ideas   5   4   3   2   1
Easy to understand,
well-organized, fun to listen to

2. Volume   5   4   3   2   1
Easy to hear;
varies volume to fit content

3. Pronunciation   5   4   3   2   1
All words are pronounced
carefully and correctly

4. Adaptation of Text to Task   5   4   3   2   1
Language, tone, and intensity
all fit the content

5. Voice   5   4   3   2   1
The voice of the author and
enthusiasm of the reader come through

6. Technology   5   4   3   2   1
All tools were used appropriately
and correctly

Scale:
5 pts = **Excellent!** No improvements needed.

4 pts = **Very good.** Only a little improvement needed.

3 pts = **Average.** This is an area to work on.

2 pts = **Below average or hardly present at all.** Needs more work.

1 pt = **Not present or unable to be heard.** Needs lots of work!

Name _____ Date _____

LIVE CHAT

Type of text: Literature or informational text

Standards addressed: Standards related to: close reading of key ideas and details in a text; drawing inferences; identifying key concepts within the text; asking questions about a text; finding answers and information within a text; getting to deeper meanings in a text; producing clear and coherent writing; effectively engaging in collaborations and discussions; presenting knowledge and ideas using a variety of components, including technology; conventions of standard English; and knowledge and use of language.

CCSS: ELA-Literacy.RL.6-8.1-8, 10; RI.6-8.1-8, 10; RH.6-8.1-8, 10; RST.6-8.1-8, 10; W.6-8.2, 4, 9, 10; WHST.6-8.2, 4, 9, 10; SL.6-8.1-2, 4, 6; L.6-8.1-3, 6

Approximate time: 10 to 30 minutes or longer

Materials and preparation: Computers and Internet access; depending on the teacher's preference, a specific app for chatting; copies of the student handout "Live-Chat Scoring Guide" (page 94)

Overview: This lesson enables students to chat live during their reading without disrupting others or the flow of the story. It works best when all people "chatting" are reading the same text in approximately the same place. Live chatting increases student motivation and engagement.

Information for teachers: Some research by the teacher is required to determine the best platform for a live chat. Some are free, while others require a paid subscription. The amount of teacher control permitted by each product also varies and should be taken into consideration. Here are a few currently available platforms: Backchannel Chat, Chatzy, TodaysMeet, and Edmodo®.

Information for teachers, continued:

The guidelines for chatting are also up to the teacher. There may be specific requirements or the lesson can be more "free form" depending on the level of the students.

Most of the platforms mentioned don't have any restrictions, so it is a good idea to review "netiquette" for chatting before students begin to chat. In a group chat, this might include:

- Include a person's name if you are responding to a specific question.

- Start a new discussion related to the reading.

- Ask questions during a discussion.

- Add thoughtful responses.

- Stay on topic.

- Don't repeat what's already been said unless you have something specific to add.

- Avoid using abbreviated texting language (Complete words and sentences are required.)

- Don't include any put-downs or inappropriate content.

- Check your spelling before you hit "send."

Strategies for differentiation: Students may want to pair up, as this lesson can be difficult for students who have poor keyboarding skills. Students can also be organized into small groups so fewer people are chatting. This strategy tends to help students who have trouble focusing on many things at once. In addition, the teacher can lower requirements for students who type slowly (for example, they might need only 5 points in a 15-minute discussion). If available, an aide, older student, or paraprofessional might type questions for students who cannot type.

Assessment: If the assignment has particular requirements about contributions to the chat, use a scoring guide like the example on page 94. Share this with students before they begin their chats. The teacher might set a certain number of points for particular grades (e.g., to earn an A, a student must gain 10 points in a 15-minute discussion).

In a free-form chat, allow students to chat about what they are reading without scoring the chat. The goal for the teacher is to gather feedback about what students are thinking and note any gaps that might need to be covered in further instruction with the whole class.

In a smaller group, students can evaluate each other during chats. Or one person can be the moderator, keeping score during the chat. (Rotate this role.) In a class discussion, the teacher can print out a transcript of the discussion and do the evaluation.

Directions for students:

Step 1   **READ:** Read the text. Stop when you are directed to do so.

Step 2   **REVIEW:** Review the requirements for your chat (if there are any) and the "Live Chat Rubric" that shows how you will be scored.

Step 3   **THINK:** Think about what you've read and what you might want to discuss with others. Plan a few ideas for conversations you can start or questions you can ask.

Step 4   **CHAT:** Contribute thoughtfully and listen carefully to what others contribute.

Example: Here's a portion of an online chat using TodaysMeet.com. The students were discussing the first act of the drama, *The Diary of Anne Frank*. (Students used their initials as their online "nicknames.")

JP: Why didn't the Franks just tell people they weren't Jewish?

JJ: The Nazis were pretty tricky about that.
I don't think they could.

LA: Who would you invite into your hiding place?

WM: Just my family. Everyone else drives me crazy.

HK: I would invite my best friends and my whole entire family.

WM: HK, what about your best friend's family?

HK: Good question. I guess there wouldn't be room
for everyone.

JJ: What would you want with you if you were in hiding for
who knows how long?

AM: Can I bring my iPad?

JJ: Not in the 1940's!!!!!

AM: I guess books since I'd have to be quiet. Maybe crossword
puzzles and stuff.

MH: JJ, do you mean if I had to hide now?

JJ: No, I mean if you were Anne Frank.

HK: I honestly don't think I would survive in hiding.
Especially with some wacky friends of my parents
like they had.

JP: I'm with you HK. Sounds like torture.

WM: Beats being in a concentration camp.

Live-Chat Scoring Guide

Students in chat group _____

Title of text _____

Name of evaluator _____ Date _____

Use this as a tally sheet, putting "tick" marks in the columns as the chat moves along. At the end, add up all the marks.

Student Handout

Student Name or Initials	Started a New Discussion +2	Asked a Thoughtful Question +2	Gave a Thoughtful Response +1	Off-Topic Comment - 1	Used Abbreviations or Texting Language - 1	Used Putdowns or Inappropriate Content -2	T O T A L

Scale: 2 points for starting a new discussion
2 points for asking a question
1 point for a thoughtful response
−1 point for off-topic comments
−1 point for using abbreviated texting language
(Whole words and sentences are required!)
−2 points for putdowns or inappropriate content

Name _____ Date _____

CHART THE CHARACTERS

Type of text: Literature or informational text that contains real-life characters (e.g., biography, memoir, narrative nonfiction, essays)

Approximate time: 20 minutes

Standards addressed: Standards related to: close reading of key ideas and details in a text; citing text to support analysis; determining central ideas; drawing inferences and conclusions; analyzing particular elements of a text; character development and analysis; writing explanatory text; producing clear and coherent writing; revising writing; effectively engaging in collaborations and discussions; conventions of standard English; and knowledge and use of language.

CCSS: ELA-Literacy.RL.6-8.1-3, 6-8, 10; RI.6-8.1-3, 6-8, 10; RH.6-8.1-3, 6-8, 10; RST.6-8.1-3, 6-8, 10; W.6-8.2, 4, 9-10; WHST.6-8.2, 4, 9-10; SL.6-8.1-4, 6; L.6-8.1-3, 6

Materials and preparation: Text or texts to be read; copies of student handout "Close-Up Look at Characters" (page 99) or of student handout "Chart the Characters" (page 100); copies of the "Character Analysis Assignment Scoring Rubric" (page 101)

Overview: This lesson is designed to help students focus on characters, character traits, and character development in a text. It also reinforces the concepts "static" (a character who doesn't change or develop) and "dynamic' (a character who undergoes an important, internal change).

Information for teachers: This lesson offers two options for character analysis lessons. Use the "Close-Up Look at Characters" student handout when individual students read different texts. Use the "Chart the Characters" handout when students have watched the same movie or read the same text.

Technology connections: This lesson can be done interactively through Google Classroom™, or using an online bulletin board, such as Padlet™.

Arts connections: After completing the chart (page 100), ask students to draw one of the characters (based on their descriptions).

Strategies for differentiation: Most differentiation will occur with the students' text selection. If they are reading at their own level, they will be able to identify characters and character traits.

Assessment: Use a simple rubric (see example on page 101) to evaluate this assignment with either of the student handouts. The teacher can evaluate student work with the rubric, or students can evaluate themselves—or both.

Directions for students:

Step 1   **READ:** As you read the text, pay close attention to characters—their traits, actions, and development.

Step 2   **WRITE:** Record your ideas and evidence for your character analysis on the handout your teacher provides.

Step 3   **SHARE:** If you read a text on your own, share with a small group your analyses of characters' traits and development and the evidence you found to support it.

Step 4   **DISCUSS:** If you read a text or watched a movie with the whole class, join in a class discussion about evidence that the text provides to support students' analyses of the different characters.

Example: Character Traits (with evidence from the text):

Students watched a YouTube video of Jon Stewart interviewing Malala Yousafzai (https://www.youtube.com /watch?v=gjGL6YY6oMs).

Here is a sample of student response and analysis of one character, Malala Yousafzai:

PHYSICAL TRAITS:

- *dark hair and eyes*
- *teenager*
- *wound on her face from an attack*
- *dressed in a bright orange head scarf*

PERSONALITY AND BEHAVIOR TRAITS:

determined and brave

- Evidence: *Her village was being attacked but she did something about it. She said, "I thought, why should I wait for someone else to help us?"*

thoughtful and peace-loving

- Evidence: *She wanted to fight back but said that would make her no better than the Taliban. She said, "You must fight others through peace and through dialogue."*

advocate for education

- Evidence: *She says the Taliban is afraid of education but she knows that that's the only way to make the world better.*

Chart the Characters, page 4

Example: Static? or Dynamic?

(with evidence from the text):
Students read the poem below, "My Teacher Took My iPod," written by Kenn Nesbitt.

My Teacher Took My iPod
by Kenn Nesbitt

My teacher took my iPod.
She said they had a rule;
I couldn't bring it into class
or even to the school.

She said she would return it;
I'd have it back that day.
But then she tried my headphones on
and gave a click on Play.

She looked a little startled,
but after just a while
she made sure we were occupied
and cracked a wicked smile.

Her body started swaying.
Her toes began to tap.
She started grooving in her seat
and rocking to the rap.

My teacher said she changed her mind.
She thinks it's now okay
to bring my iPod into class.
She takes it every day.

Here is a sample of student response to the question of whether the character development was static or dynamic for each character:

The narrator's character is **static.** ***Evidence:*** *He (or she) stays consistent throughout the poem, loves to use an iPod, and breaks the class rule.*

The teacher's character is **dynamic.** ***Evidence:*** *She takes the iPod away because it's against the rules, but after she tries it herself, she likes it and uses it. The text also says "My teacher said she changed her mind."*

Close-Up Look at Characters

Title of text:_____

A. Character's name

_____

1ˢᵗ character trait

Evidence from the story:

2ⁿᵈ character trait

Evidence from the story:

Draw the character, or an item associated with him or her.

B. Character's name

_____

1ˢᵗ character trait

Evidence from the story:

2ⁿᵈ character trait

Evidence from the story:

Draw the character, or an item associated with him or her.

Name _____   Date _____

Chart the Characters

Use this organizing tool to record character traits as you watch, listen to, or read a text with several characters.

Title of text _____

Character Names	Physical Traits ▼	Personality Traits ▼	Static or Dynamic? Evidence? ▼	Other Notes
_____				
_____				
_____				
_____				
_____				

Name _____ Date _____

Character Analysis Assignment
Scoring Rubric

Title of text _____

Student Handout

	Advanced Score = 4	Proficient Score = 3	Partially Proficient Score = 2	Unsatisfactory Score = 1
Completion	All portions filled in completely	80 to 99% complete	70 to 79% complete	Less than 70% complete
Accuracy	All portions accurate	80 to 99% accurate	70 to 79% accurate	Less than 70% of responses are accurate
Evidence	All responses have compelling, supporting evidence	Most responses have compelling, supporting evidence	Most responses have supporting evidence	Less than 70% of responses have supporting evidence
Presentation	Spelling and grammar are correct; shows pride in work	Most spelling and grammar are correct	Contains many errors	Hard to understand or decode

Completion _____ score   Evidence _____ score

Accuracy _____ score   Presentation _____ score

Comments:

Name _____ Date _____

JOURNALING
(VOCABULARY INCLUDED)

Type of text: Literature or informational text

Standards addressed: Standards related to: close reading of key ideas and details in a text; citing text to support analysis; determining theme or central ideas; providing a summary of the text; drawing inferences or conclusions; analyzing the meaning of certain text events, characters, or developments; writing argumentative, informational, explanatory, or narrative text; producing clear and coherent writing; engaging in collaborations and discussions; vocabulary acquisitions and use; conventions of standard English; and knowledge and use of language. *Note: The journaling assignments can focus on any additional literacy standards the teacher chooses.*

CCSS: Possible coverage of all reading and writing standards: ELA-Literacy.RL.6-8.1-10; RI.6-8.1-10; RH.6-8.1-10; RST.6-8.10; W.6-8.1-10; WHST.6-8.1-10; L.6-8.1-6

Approximate lesson time: Varies according to assigned requirements

Materials and preparation: Text; physical notebook, computer "notebook" file, or website dedicated to journaling; copies of teacher-prepared journal assignments and accompanying rubrics (see examples of journal requirement templates for informational text and literature on pages 106 and 107)

Overview: This lesson models a process whereby students stop at a set point in their reading and reflect on what they've read as well as focus on some of the critical vocabulary in the set portion of the text.

Information for teachers: This lesson can be incorporated at any time during a class period or during the reading of the text. The teacher sets the journal-entry requirements according to the text and may require students to journal every 30 minutes, or every 20 pages in a book, or every chapter. Additionally, the teacher can decide the journal format and specific journal assignments. (See sample assignments on pages 104 and 105.) Do require all types of writing over the school year, including argument or opinion, informational, and narrative.

Technology connections: This lesson works as well as an online blog as it does on paper.

Arts connections: Where appropriate, illustrations or other graphics can be added as a requirement for a journal assignment.

Strategies for differentiation: Some students may require a shortened version of the assignment. Students who struggle with reading tasks may need an assignment template rather than a blank page. Advanced readers can be challenged through the choice of text to be read. Students who have difficulty with writing a journal entry might be given the option of oral journaling—dictating to a recording device or to a helper who will transcribe for them.

Assessment: The sample templates for journal requirements (on pages 106 and 107) each include a simple assessment rubric. Students can review the rubric criteria before writing journal entries and teachers can evaluate students after assignment completion, or students can use the rubric for self-assessment.

Directions for students:

Step 1   **READ:** Read the assigned text or portion of the text.

Step 2   **THINK:** Think about what you've read. Pay attention to unfamiliar words and phrases.

Step 3   **WRITE:** Write your journal entry based on the requirements.

Step 4   **DRAW or DEPICT:** Draw or otherwise depict your "entry" for one part of the assignment, if you can.

Examples: See the requirements on the sample journal assignments (pages 106-107). The examples here and on page 105 are excerpts from real student journal entries in response to five different texts. Students pasted a copy of the requirements and rubrics into their physical or electronic notebooks.

Text #1: Article from Scholastic Action Magazine

Source: Schotz, Jenn. "Should Kids Play Football?" *Action*. Jefferson City, MO: Scholastic, Inc. September 7, 2015, p. 22-3. Online at http://action.scholastic.com/issues/09_07_15/book#/1

Journal Entry—Plot Summary:

This article presents two sides of the argument about the safety of kids playing football. It gives reasons why it's too risky and reasons why it's not too risky and asks the reader to decide for him or herself.

Text #2: Song lyrics from Taylor Swift's "Shake It Off"

Source: Available at http://www.directlyrics.com/taylor-swift-shake-it-off-lyrics.html

Journal Entry—One-Sentence Opinion:

I think this song is very inspirational, especially to teenagers, because it reminds us that sometimes we just have to ignore bad things that happen and move on.

Text #3: A World Book Article about Cryosurgery

Source: Available at http://worldbookonline.com/student/article?id=ar142470#tab=home
page

Journal Entry—Five New Vocabulary Words:

1. **cryosurgery** – *surgery using intense cold to freeze and destroy damaged tissues*
2. **cryogens** – *substances that reach very low temperatures, including liquid nitrogen, carbon dioxide, and others*
3. **cryoprobe** – *a needlelike device with a cryogen inside it*
4. **invasive** – *something that invades (goes in)*
5. **pigmentation** – *the coloring of an object, such as the color, or* pigmentation, *of skin*

Source: Available at:

http://worldbookonline.com/wbtimelines/viewtimelines?source=WB&timelineId=54a7114 ee4b09e8509209fe9

Journal Entry—Five New Things I Learned:

1. *Stand Watie (a Cherokee) was the first and only Indian brigadier general in the Confederate Army during the American Civil War.*
2. *In 1868 the Fort Laramie Treaty was signed, creating a reservation in the Dakota Territory. The treaty was broken by the government when gold was found in the Black Hills.*
3. *In 1869, a Pawnee scout named Traveling Bear became the first Native American awarded the Medal of Honor.*
4. *The Battle of Little Bighorn happened in 1876, and General Custer was killed along with 250 of his soldiers.*
5. *Will Rogers was partly of Cherokee ancestry.*

Text #5: Comedy Video from YouTube: Key & Peele's "TeachingCenter" (a satire of "SportsCenter")

Source: Available at https://youtu.be/dkHqPFbxmOU

Journal Entry—Basic Facts about Setting and Characters:

The setting of this video is a studio called "TeachingCenter" that's a copy of SportsCenter. It has clips from schools and from draft day. There are two reporters at a desk talking to the camera.

The characters are giving a form of news about teachers as if the teachers were professional athletes. It has a lot of irony and humor, including commentary about teachers' skills and salaries.

Reading Journal Requirements
Informational Text

How many pages does your text have? _____   Divide this by 8 = _____

When you finish _____ number of pages, complete a journal entry.

Student
Handout

Requirements:

Summary of what you read (50 words or fewer)

Five new things you learned

Five vocabulary words that were new to you (and their meanings)

Three questions you have about what you read

One-sentence opinion of what you read

Rubric for Evaluation:

	Advanced 4	Proficient 3	Partially Proficient 2	Unsatisfactory 1
Ideas	Meets or exceeds all requirements; information is complete and accurate	Meets all requirements; information is accurate	Meets 70 to 80% of requirements; most information is accurate	Many inaccuracies or fails to meet 70% of requirements
Voice	Work is thoughtful and unique, and expresses individuality	Work is thoughtful and unique	Work is thoughtful	Work doesn't show individuality
Conventions and Presentation	No errors; shows pride in work	A few errors that don't interfere with meaning; shows pride in work	Errors that interfere with meaning and/ or make the work hard to read	Illegible in places

Total _____

Name _____   Date _____

Reading Journal Requirements
Literature

How many pages does your text have? _____ Divide this by 8 = _____

When you finish _____ number of pages, complete a journal entry.

Student Handout

Requirements:

Basic facts about setting and characters

Plot summary (50 words or fewer)

Five words that were new, different, or exciting
   (and their meanings)

Three questions you have about what you read

One-sentence opinion of what you read

Rubric for Evaluation:

	Advanced 4	Proficient 3	Partially Proficient 2	Unsatisfactory 1
Ideas	Meets or exceeds all requirements; information is complete and accurate	Meets all requirements; information is accurate	Meets 70 to 80% of requirements; most information is accurate	Many inaccuracies or fails to meet 70% of requirements
Voice	Work is thoughtful and unique, and expresses individuality	Work is thoughtful and unique	Work is thoughtful	Work doesn't show individuality
Conventions and Presentation	No errors; shows pride in work	A few errors that don't interfere with meaning; shows pride in work	Errors that interfere with meaning and/ or make the work hard to read	Illegible in places

Total _____

Name _____ Date _____

CLASS QUILT

Type of text: Literary or nonfiction narrative

Standards addressed: Standards related to: close examination of key ideas and details; drawing inferences; drawing conclusions; identifying the theme of a text; communicating themes and key ideas from texts; integrating visual information with print or digital text information; determining meanings of words and phrases as they are used in a text; acquiring and using vocabulary; effectively engaging in collaborations and discussions; conventions of standard English; and knowledge and use of language.

CCSS: ELA-Literacy RL.6-8.1-4, 7, 10; RI.1-4, 7, 10; RH.1-4, 7, 10; RST.1-4, 7, 10; W.6-8.9, 10; WHST.6-8.9, 10; SL.6-8.1-6; L.6-8.1-6

Approximate lesson time: 30 to 40 minutes

Materials and preparation: Text; paper cut to resemble quilt pieces (can be construction paper, blank note cards, or the students can cut their own shapes); colored pencils or markers; copies of "Quilt-Square Rubric" (page 111)

Overview: This lesson is designed to give students an experience in visually representing a text's theme.

Information for teachers: In this lesson, students focus on identifying the theme or themes of a text. As a group, the students agree on a theme. Each individual then chooses a word that captures or expresses an aspect of the theme from all or part of the text. Each student then creates a quilt square to show a visual depiction of the word and the concept represented. In the end, the squares are assembled to make a large quilt. See examples of finished quilts on page 110.

Technology connections: Quilt squares can be made using a drawing app or program such as Drawing Pad™ or Creative Book Builder™. The squares can be printed and displayed, or they can be assembled electronically on a bulletin board format (Padlet™ or Pinterest®).

Arts connections: To inspire students, the teacher can show examples of works of art related to the text or its theme. In addition, students can listen to appropriate music as they create their quilt squares. (In the case of the example on page 110, students listened to slave songs and celebratory anthems related to freedom.)

Strategies for differentiation: Teachers can offer a word list for students who struggle to choose a word for their quilts. It is also helpful if the class brainstorms words together to generate ideas for all students.

Assessment: The teacher or students (or both) can use a rubric such as the one on page 111 to evaluate finished quilt squares.

Directions for students:

Step 1 **THINK:** Brainstorm words that mean the same or approximately the same as the theme of your text.

Step 2 **CREATE and COLOR:** Choose your favorite word, then make a quilt square that contains both your word and pictures or symbols to visually depict the word. Quilt squares should be colorful and words should be easy to read from a distance.

Step 3 **ASSEMBLE:** Add your square to the quilt. Squares may be sewn together or stapled to a bulletin board or wall, or—to save them for the future—glue squares onto large pieces of butcher paper. The finished product will look more "quilt-like" if the squares are assembled facing different directions.

Example: A group of eighth-grade students had read the first half of Julius Lester's *To Be a Slave*. Each student thought of or found another word for "slavery" and made a quilt square based on that word. The squares were all contributed to one quilt. At the end of the story, the process was repeated for the word "freedom," resulting in two contrasting quilts.

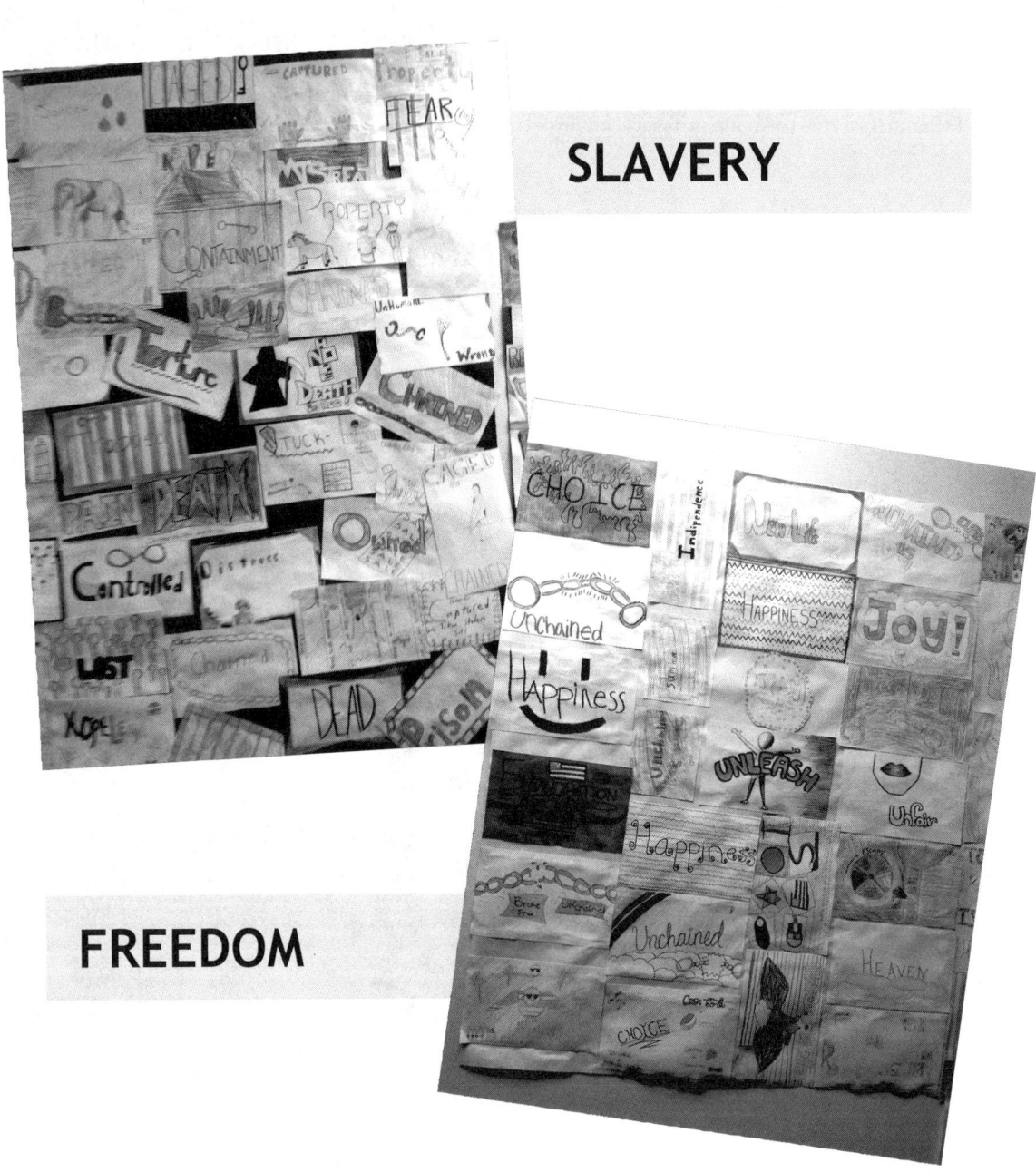

SLAVERY

FREEDOM

Quilt-Square Rubric

Student name _____ Date _____

Theme of quilt _____

Evaluator _____

Student Handout

Criteria Elements	Advanced 9 to 10 pts	Proficient 8 pts	Partially Proficient 7 pts	Unsatisfactory 0 to 6 pts
Ideas	Makes audience think; has a good variety of ideas and representations; says something meaningful about you	Makes audience think; has some variety of ideas and representations; says something meaningful about you	Somewhat thoughtful; has a little variety of ideas and representations; shows an attempt to reveal a personal response to the theme	Ordinary; little or no thought-provoking elements
Visual Appeal	Fun to look at; WOW!	Fun to look at; put together well	Some parts are hard to understand	Quilt square is hard to read or understand
Originality	Original ideas; different from other quilt squares	Original ideas; mostly different from other quilt squares	Some original ideas; somewhat different from other quilt squares	Ordinary or similar to many others' squares

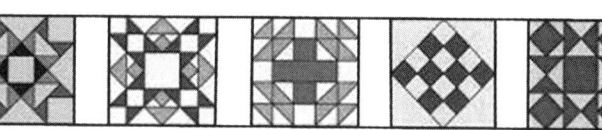

Total = ____/30

Name _____ Date _____

PART 3
LESSONS
AFTER
READING

So her strong young mind continued to grow,
nurtured by the voices of all those authors
who had sent their books out into
the world like ships on the sea.

~Roald Dahl (Matilda)

Contents

The descriptor "Lessons After Reading" is not exclusive. Many of these lessons work as well in the middle of a text as they do at the end. So "after" in a particular case might mean "at the end" of whatever text portion comprises the assignment.

Most lessons in this section assume that "READ" is the first step and has been completed, so "READ" generally is not specified as Step 1 in the student directions. Even though "READ" may not refer to a complete book, article, poem, play, or other text, remember that many literacy skills are honed best when students work with short texts.

Each lesson is designed to meet specific standards while doing one or more of these things:

- Increase comprehension of fiction and nonfiction
- Help students look at what they've read in a new way
- Improve summarization skills
- Improve ability to provide evidence in support of their conclusions, through both research and inference
- Help students analyze the various components of texts
- Improve discussion, collaboration, and presentation skills

As with the lessons in the first two sections of this book, these are designed to give the teacher many options within the lesson format set by the book.

TEXT MAPS TO ANALYZE THE BASICS

Type of text: Literature or informational text

Standards addressed: Standards related to: close reading of key ideas and details in a text; identifying main ideas and key events; drawing inferences and conclusions; analyzing particular structural elements of a text; integrating elements of a text; citing evidence from the text to support conclusions and analysis; summarizing a text; examining the structure of text and analyzing its effects on the meaning or message; representing text structure visually; understanding and analyzing uses and effects of vocabulary in the text; communicating understandings of text meaning and organization; producing clear and coherent writing; effectively engaging in collaborations and discussions; conventions of standard English; and knowledge and use of language.

CCSS: ELA-Literacy RL.6-8.1-5, 7-10; RI.6-8.1-5, 7-10; RH.6-8.1-5, 7-10; RST.6-8.1-5, 7-10; W.6-8.4, 6, 9-10; WHST.6-8.4, 6, 9-10; SL.6-8.1-6; L.6-8.1-6

Approximate lesson time: 30 to 40 minutes

Materials and preparation: Text(s); copies of appropriate text map template (pages 117-119); copies of "Text-Map Rubric" (page 120)

Overview: This lesson is designed to help students analyze the components of a text and represent them graphically.

Information for teachers: The idea of a text map is to show students that all texts have commonalities as well as unique components. Notice that this lesson includes three different text-map templates: two for fiction (or narrative nonfiction) and one for informational text. Students can gather in small groups to show and explain their text maps. Make sure students understand that narrative nonfiction tells a story—a story that is as true and accurate as possible.

For an extension of text mapping, students can map a fiction and a nonfiction text on a similar topic and compare the text structures.

Technology connections: The text-map templates can be provided online where students can complete them. This enables students to collaborate and share their final products.

Arts connections: Once students have practiced using text maps, encourage them to design their own graphic presentation of text elements. Provide the list of items, questions, or elements to be included (or let the students choose which elements to include) before they begin.

Strategies for differentiation: Some students may not be familiar with the idea of a text map. To support such students, it is beneficial to create a map as a whole class activity before students make their own. The easiest way to do this is to read a short picture book aloud (provided it has all the required components) and demonstrate to the whole class how to create a text map from that simple book. Beyond that, differing student book choices will allow students to complete the task with texts at their own levels.

Assessment: A simple rubric is provided for review and evaluation of text maps. The teacher, the student, a peer, or any combination of these can serve as the evaluator(s).

Directions for students:

Step 1   **PREPARE:** Review the text-map template that you will be completing after you read the text.

Step 2   **READ:** Read the entire text assigned for this lesson.

Step 3   **WRITE:** Fill in the text map after you read.

Step 4   **SHARE:** Share your text map with your group and explain your evidence.

Step 5   **RESPOND:** Use the "Text-Map Rubric" to give feedback to classmates about their text maps and their presentations of the maps.

Text Map III Example:

Text: an online article about cicadas (Full page sample of student-completed Text Map III handout.)

Text Map III: Informational Text

Text "17-Year Old Cicadas Are Buzzing In! What to Expect." Author _Livescience.com. April 17, 2013_

Student Handout

Summarize the main topic and the purpose of the text:

The author explains what happens when the cicadas emerge every 17 years and why the insects' cycle takes so long.

List all the subtopics:

overpopulation, cicada predators, the cicada cycle, sound of the cicadas, hibernation

What organizational tools are found in the text?

captions, bold subtitles, links to explanatory topics, quotations from scientists

How are these helpful?

They make the reading easier and the details more understandable. The links provide a lot more interesting information about the cicadas and their cycle and behavior.

What graphics or other media accompany the text? How are these helpful?

photographs, cycle diagrams, historical chart of emergence, sound recording of the cicada noise
They give even more information, a feel for what it is like when the cicadas emerge, and an idea of the intensity of the cicada sound!

What vocabulary clues help to increase your understanding?

racket, like a muffled burglar alarm, pesky, invasion, infestation, irritating, humming

A question you still have about the topic:

What more do scientists know about the 17-year life underground?

Name _____ Date _____

THEME

Individuality

vs.

Conformity

EVIDENCE

"We did not know what to make of her. In our minds we tried to pin her to a corkboard like a butterfly, but the pin merely went through and away she flew."
(page 97)

"She looked magnificently, wonderfully, gloriously ordinary. She looked like a hundred other girls at Mica High."
(page 140)

Text Map I Example:

Text: the novel *Stargirl*, by Jerry Spinelli (Theme and Evidence boxes show a sample of student-completed portion of Part D on Text Map I handout.)

Text Map I: Fiction or Narrative Nonfiction

Text _____   Author _____

Student Handout

A. **Major conflict** in the story:

Cite a line that gives evidence of this.

B. Two **important events** in the story:

1. _____
   Evidence of its importance:

2. _____
   Evidence of its importance:

C. Brief description of **story conclusion**:

Was the ending effective? Why or why not?

Theme

Evidence

D. **Theme**
Write the theme (author's main message, meaning, or lesson) in the arrow. In the rectangle, give a detail or quote as evidence showing that this is the theme.

Name _____   Date _____

Text Map II: Fiction or Narrative Nonfiction

Text _____ Author _____

Student
Handout

One of the key SETTINGS in this text:

Evidence of its importance:

Two key details about the main CHARACTER:

1. _____

    Evidence of its importance:

2. _____

    Evidence of its importance:

PLOT

What happens in the beginning? (PLOT)

What happens in the middle? (PLOT)

What happens at the end? (PLOT)

Name _____ Date _____

Text Map III: Informational Text

Text _____ Author _____

Student Handout

Summarize the **main topic** and the **purpose** of the text:	What **organizational tools** are found in the text? **How are these helpful?**
List all the **subtopics:**	

What **graphics** or other media accompany the text? How are these helpful?

What **vocabulary** clues help to increase your understanding?	A **question** you still have about the topic:

Name _____ Date _____

Text-Map Rubric

	Advanced 4	Proficient 3	Partially Proficient 2	Unsatisfactory 1
Completion	All portions filled in completely	80 to 99% filled in	70 to 79% filled in	Less than 70% complete
Accuracy	All portions accurate	80 to 99% accurate	70 to 79% accurate	Less than 70% of responses are accurate
Evidence	All responses have compelling, supporting evidence	Most responses have compelling, supporting evidence	Most responses have supporting evidence	Less than 70% of responses have supporting evidence
Presentation	Spelling and grammar are correct, showing pride in work	Most spelling and grammar are correct	Contains many errors	Hard to understand and/or decode

Date_____

Student _____

Evaluator _____

My Score

_____

of 16

Name _____   Date _____

NARRATIVE SPEECHES

Type of text: Literature

Standards addressed: Standards related to: close reading of key ideas and details in a text; identifying main ideas and key events; drawing inferences and conclusions; finding evidence from the text to support conclusions and analysis; analyzing characters, their interaction with story events and other characters, and their roles in furthering the story and meaning; summarizing; identifying and comparing points of view; writing narratives; producing clear and coherent writing; preparing and delivering a speech; effectively engaging in collaborations and discussions; evaluating a speaker's presentation; conventions of standard English; and knowledge and use of language.

CCSS: ELA-Literacy RL.6-8.1-3, 6-7, 9-10; W.6-8.3-4, 8-10; WHST.6-8.3-4, 8-10; SL.6-8.1-6; L.6-8.1-3, 6

Approximate lesson time: Two to three class periods (not including presentation time)

Materials and preparation: Text(s); copies of student handouts "Narrative-Speech Assignment" (page 124), "Narrative-Speech Planning Guide" (page 125), and "Narrative-Speech Evaluation" (page 126)

Overview: This lesson gives students a chance to take the perspective of a character from a literary text. Students use specific details from the text to give a speech or presentation from their character's point of view, complete with realistic details.

Information for teachers: This works best when students are given a wide variety of choices to avoid repetitive speeches. In the example provided on page 123, students were participating in book groups. Each student in the group chose a different character, so no two speeches were the same. Students were allowed to fill in details of their character's life as long as they were true to both the facts in the text and the spirit of the text.

Technology connections: Students can record the speeches and play them as videos for the class, or share them widely in various formats or settings. They can also make and project backdrops or slides to enhance their presentations.

Arts connections: Encourage students to add costumes, props, or backdrops to their presentations.

Strategies for differentiation: Some differentiation will be built into the assignment based on the students' choices of both texts and characters within the chosen texts. In addition, teachers can provide scaffolding for students in need of more structure to help them prepare to be the character. Do this by creating a planning sheet where students make notes to answer such questions as these—taking on the role of the chosen character.

What is your name?	*Do you have enemies? If yes, who are they?*
What do you look like?	*Tell about your most exciting day…*
How old are you?	*Of what are you afraid?*
Where do you live?	*What are your goals?*
What is your life like?	*What do you think will happen in your future?*
What is going well for you?	*What conflicts exist in your life?*
What is your biggest challenge?	*How would you describe your personality?*

Assessment: Use an evaluation form such as the "Narrative-Speech Evaluation" on page 126. The teacher, a peer, or the speaker (or any combination of these) can serve as evaluators. As an option, you might copy the evaluation form on both sides of a paper so that two evaluators can provide feedback on the same sheet.

Directions for students:

Step 1 **GET READY:** Carefully read the information and directions found in the handouts "Narrative-Speech Assignment" and "Narrative-Speech Planning Guide."

Step 2 **PREPARE:** Plan and outline your speech or presentation using the "Narrative-Speech Planning Guide."

Step 3 **PRACTICE:** Rehearse your speech or presentation.

Step 4 **DELIVER:** Present your speech to the group.

Example: Students completed this lesson after they read a variety of historical fiction books as part of a unit on United States History—Westward Expansion. These are some of the characters students chose for narrative speeches:

Daniel from *Cabin on Trouble Creek* (J. Van Leewen, 2004)

Emmy from *The Quilt Walk* (S. Dallas, 2012)

Francis from *Mr. Tucket* (G. Paulsen, 2000)

Caddie from *Caddie Woodlawn* (C. R. Brink, 1935)

Georgie from *One Came Home* (A. Timberlake, 2013)

Gil from *The Oxbow Incident* (W. Van Tilburg Clark, 1940)

Excerpts from a student speaking as Lucy from *The Ballad of Lucy Whipple* (K. Cushman, 1996)

My name is California Morning Whipple, and I was born in 1836 in Massachusetts. After being forced to move to the real California, I decided that I didn't want to be named after a place full of dust and bad smells so I changed my name to Lucy in 1849.

A good thing about being me is that I'm pretty smart and I'm very independent. I drive my mom crazy by being so independent. A problematic thing about being me is that I have lots of trouble being happy with what I have, and I'm always looking for something different.

Narrative-Speech Assignment for Book Groups

Student Handout

Information: For this assignment, you will be preparing and giving a three- to five-minute speech from the perspective of a character in your book. You may choose a major or minor character; each person in your group needs to choose a different character.

Here are the steps for success:

1. CHOOSE
a character from your story.

2. BRAINSTORM
all the facts about your character that you can include. Check your book for accuracy.

3. INFER
details about your character and fill in any details you think would be interesting to the audience. The details about your character must be REALISTIC and BELIEVABLE. Make your character "come alive"! Focus on what makes the character different. Is it the character's personality? Is it that the character likes to eat something unusual? Is it the fact that your character plays the guitar but does it in secret? Is it the character's habit of not telling the truth? Is it the character's delight in tricking people? Is it the curious fact that she changed her name? Be creative!

4. PLAN
your speeches. Each individual should include the required content shown on the "Narrative-Speech Planning Guide" student handout.

5. PERFORM
Now you're ready to **become** this character and **tell your story** to the class in the form of a first-person narrative speech!

Name _____   Date _____

Narrative-Speech Planning Guide

Student Handout

Your speech will be graded on **content** and **delivery**.

Here are the requirements:

Content:

Introduction
- Who are you?

Body
- What things have you seen during your life?

- What is it like to be in your situation?

- What are good things and some things about you that are challenging?

- Remember to include facts, details, and examples that make you seem realistic.

NOTE: Be consistent in your organization. If you are talking about "a day in the life..." then stick to that. If you want to talk about your whole life, then divide it up logically.

Conclusion
- Sum up your situation, philosophy of life, or future plans.

Delivery:
- Proper length of three to five minutes
- Outstanding poise, eye contact, volume, and rate
- Enthusiasm!

Name _____ Date _____

Narrative-Speech Evaluation

Speaker _____ Date _____

Evaluator _____

Student Handout

Approach to front of class; ready to go	1	2	3	4	5
Posture; poise; confidence	1	2	3	4	5
Eye contact	1	2	3	4	5
Volume; projection	1	2	3	4	5
Rate of speech	1	2	3	4	5
Vocal expression; enthusiasm	1	2	3	4	5

Introduction

Attention-getter	1	2	3	4	5
Background information	1	2	3	4	5
Preview; statement of purpose	1	2	3	4	5

Body

Appropriate facts and details	1	2	3	4	5
Realistic character	1	2	3	4	5
Variety of interesting information	1	2	3	4	5
Logical organization	1	2	3	4	5
Sufficient facts and details	1	2	3	4	5
Consistent characterization	1	2	3	4	5

Conclusion

Satisfying wrap-up	1	2	3	4	5
Audience is taken into consideration	1	2	3	4	5
Listened courteously to other speeches	1	2	3	4	5

Key

5 = advanced; exceeded requirements

4 = proficient; met all requirements

3 = partially proficient; met 50 to 75% of requirements

2 = unsatisfactory; met less than 50% of requirements

1 = did not attempt to meet requirements

Met time requirement? _____ yes (+10)   _____ no (-10)

TOTAL SCORE = _____ of 100

Name _____ Date _____

EXPERT CONVERSATIONS

Type of text: Informational text or other nonfiction text

Standards addressed: Standards related to: close reading of key ideas and details in a text; finding information; drawing inferences and conclusions; summarizing information; finding textual evidence to support conclusions and analysis; researching to expand understanding of topic; comparing points of view; writing argumentative, informational, or explanatory text; producing clear and coherent writing; planning a conversation; effectively engaging in collaborations and discussions; using technology to communicate effectively; evaluating a speaker's presentation; vocabulary acquisition and use; conventions of standard English; and knowledge and use of language.

CCSS: ELA-Literacy RI.6-8.1-4, 6-10; RH.6-8.W.6-8.1-4, 6-10; RST.6-8. 1-4, 6-10; W.6-8.1-2, 4, 6-10; WHST.6-8.1-2, 4, 6-10; SL.6-8.1, 4-6; L.6-8.1-6

Approximate lesson time: Anywhere from one to four class periods, depending on the specific assignment

Materials and preparation: Text(s); access to technology (for the research, conversation, and product)—dependent on the details of the assignment; copies of student handouts "Expert-Profile Sheet and Planner" (page 130) and "Expert-Conversation Evaluation" (page 131)

Overview: In this lesson, students become an "expert" on a topic from a nonfiction text. Then they communicate with a "non-expert" (may or may not be from the same grade) via postcards, letters, podcasts, online chats, or social networking.

Information for teachers: This lesson helps students understand point of view, audience, and voice. It also reinforces the skills of research, summarizing, and making inferences. It also helps students polish and deepen communication skills of writing, speaking, listening—within conventional platforms of postcards or letters or e-mail or other online platforms. This is a great lesson for polishing argumentation—as "experts" can present arguments to defend a major theory, cause, or viewpoint.

Arts connections: If the platform makes this possible, "experts" can share drawings, diagrams, illustrations, or videos to answer questions and communicate information.

Strategies for differentiation: The depth and breadth of this lesson are virtually endless. The level of difficulty can be adjusted for students of all skills. Students who struggle with the research and preparation tasks may need help filling out the "Expert-Profile Sheet and Planner" prior to beginning the conversation. Some differentiation will occur with the selection of the topic as well.

Assessment: The person interviewing the expert or the teacher can be the evaluator, using the "Expert-Conversation Evaluation" (page 131). If the interview takes place in front of the class, it is easy for a peer or the teacher to complete the evaluation. If students record their interviews on a video camera, smartphone, or tablet, they can email their conversations to the teacher for evaluation. (This option allows students to edit interviews before submitting them.) If interviews are electronic, the class or smaller groups can watch them at a later time and use the scoring guide to evaluate.

Directions for students:

Step 1   **CHOOSE:** Select a topic from your reading. You will become an "expert" on this topic, so choose carefully!

Step 2   **RESEARCH:** Do enough research to become well versed in your topic. Take notes from each source, and organize your notes by various subtopics.

Step 3   **WRITE:** Fill out the "Expert-Profile Sheet and Planner" for yourself as the expert. Use information from the text as well as research and your own inferences and experiences.

Step 4   **COMMUNICATE:** Find a partner and start a two-way conversation. You and your partner may decide to write letters (on paper or online with such an online platform as ePals, Schoololgy®, or KidLink.org) or use a social media platform (Facebook®, Google Chat™, etc.). Please check the evaluation form to see how your work will be assessed.

Examples:

Seventh-graders in a Social Studies class learned about Mexico, reading various articles and information about the country and its people. Each student chose a specific topic (such as Mexican cities, landmarks, government, history, food, art, clothing, religion, holidays, and the sport of bullfighting) and researched it to become an "expert" on that topic. Each student then partnered with a second grader whose class was also studying Mexico to have a conversation.

Here is an excerpt of a conversation between Brad (grade 7) and Jenna (grade 2). Brad's new name was Dr. Pollo, MFE (Mexican Food Expert).

Brad: *Hello. I am Dr. Pollo, MFE. How can I help you?*

Jenna: *What is your favorite food?*

Brad: *Here in Mexico we love to make tortillas from either corn or flour. They are like flat bread that we can put fillings into.*

Jenna: *Do you eat the same food we have in America?*

Brad: *Yes, Jenna. We have lots of the same food. Because of our hot weather, we can grow lots of fruits like avocados, bananas, and mangoes. In fact, lots of Americans get their fruit from right here in Mexico.*

Jenna: *How does it get to the United States?*

Brad: *Usually on trucks!*

Jenna: *What is* case-o? *I heard that word in a restaurant.*

Brad: *I think you're talking about* **queso**. *It's our word for* **cheese.**

Here are some other "experts" that developed in other classes:

- an archaeologist who explains what she does in her job

- a mathematician like Sophie Germain who answered questions about her contributions to mathematics

- an inventor like Ruth Graves Wakefield (who invented the chocolate chip cookie at the Toll House Inn) who answered questions about her invention and about being an inventor

Expert-Profile Sheet and Planner

Student Handout

Your name:

Your official expert title:

Your area of expertise:

Sources consulted to build your knowledge:

General description of new things you learned:

Your conversation partner's name: _____

Format or platform used to converse: _____

What you need to consider about your partner before you start: _____
(Hint: he or she is your audience.)
_____

Now you're ready to converse! If you don't know the answer to something, it's okay to say that—then conduct additional research as needed.

Name _____   Date _____

Expert-Conversation Evaluation

Speaker _____ Date _____

Partner's namer _____

Ideas   4   3   2   1
Accurate, interesting, varied conversation;
expert contributes at least five separate facts

Student Handout

Word Choice   4   3   2   1
Words are accurate, specific,
appropriate, and precise

Voice   4   3   2   1
Consistently projects expert's
point of view

Total = _____ of 24

Communication of Ideas   4   3   2   1
Communicates clearly at a level
understandable by the partner

Conventions   4   3   2   1
Nearly error free, accurate
pronunciation or spelling and punctuation

Staple your planning sheet to this sheet.

Visuals   4   3   2   1
Recordings or informational visuals are of
good quality and add to the understanding of the topic

KEY
4 = Advanced; exceeds requirements and demonstrates mastery of skill
3 = Proficient; meets the standard and demonstrates command of the skill
2 = Partially Proficient; meets part of the criteria with some deficiencies
1 = Unsatisfactory; meets less than 70% of the criteria

Name _____ Date _____

BE THE CHARACTER!

Type of text: Literature or informational text

Standards addressed: Standards related to: close reading of key ideas and details in a text; drawing inferences and conclusions; summarizing information; finding evidence from the text to support conclusions and analysis; character development and analysis; identifying and comparing points of view; researching to expand understanding of topic; taking notes; planning and executing the steps of a project; giving an oral presentation; presenting with visual aids; evaluating a speaker's presentation; conventions of standard English; and knowledge and use of language.

CCSS: ELA-Literacy RI.6-8.1-4, 6-7, 10; RH.6-8.W.6-8.1-4, 6-7, 10; RST.6-8.1-2, 4, 6-7, 10; W.6-8.4, 6-10; WHST.6-8.4, 6-10; SL.6-8.1-6; L.6-8.1-3, 6

Approximate lesson time: A minimum of one class period for preparation and one to two for presentations

Materials and preparation: Text; copies of student handouts "Be the Character! Rubric" (page 135) and "Be the Character! Assignment Guide" (pages 136-137); Internet access and other materials for research; materials for individual students as needed for projects

Overview: This lesson encourages students to use a combination of facts and inferences to put themselves in the figurative shoes of a character. Each student does research to broaden the picture of the character's life, culture, circumstances, and time period, and then translates that understanding into a project that showcases the character's life, accomplishments, or culture.

Information for teachers: This lesson is especially fun with historical characters and time periods, but works well for many fictional and nonfictional characters and time periods—including current ones. The project can be virtually unlimited or more restricted, depending on the available materials. In the example shown on page 134, students are given a choice to create or find, explain, and demonstrate (or otherwise share) one of these related to a character from their text: costume, accessory, cooking, or music.

Arts connections: This project makes an excellent interdisciplinary assignment or even the basis for an entire unit. Work with art, music, and family and consumer sciences teachers to give students more specific instruction and guidelines on building, designing, cooking, performing, or music making.

Strategies for differentiation: The project can be limited to just one element, expanded to allow for design of several or all of the choices that would showcase a character, or adapted to include ideas students suggest or find in their research.

Assessment: A wide variety of assessments can be used to evaluate or respond to student projects. This is highly dependent upon the precise project requirements set for students. A simple rubric is provided on page 135. It can be used to evaluate or respond to projects of many different kinds.

Directions for students:

Step 1 **ANALYZE:** Choose a character from your reading and follow the questions on your "Be the Character! Assignment" to analyze some character features.

Step 2 **CHOOSE:** Select a project that shows something about the character's life, work, or accomplishments. Choose something that your character would use or do and enjoy presenting.

Step 3 **RESEARCH:** Do whatever research you need in order to create your project with as much accuracy as possible. Take notes as you research.

Step 4 **DESIGN and CREATE:** Gather materials that you need and create your project. Refer to the "Be a Character! Rubric" as you work.

Step 5 **PRESENT:** Demonstrate, show, or otherwise share your project with the group. Be sure to communicate the connection between the text you read, the character, and the project.

Be the Character!, page 3

Examples:  As part of a unit on Colonial America, students made a project based on a historical fiction or nonfiction book they read. In addition to colonial figures from biographies, students chose characters from such novels as *Johnny Tremain* (Johnny, Cilla, Rab), *Chains* (Isabel, Curzon, Ruth), *Witch Child* (Mary, Eliza, Jaybird), *Beyond the Burning Time* (Mary, John Proctor, Captain Coatsworth), *The Ransom of Mercy Carter* (Mercy, Tannhahorens), *Cast Two Shadows* (Caroline, Georgia Ann, Sarah), *The Witch of Blackbird Pond* (Hannah, Nathaniel, Katherine), *Hope's Crossing* (Noah, Hope), *Fever 1793* (Matilda, Nathaniel), and *Sarah Bishop* (Sarah).

Student projects included:

- drawings or replicas of colonial-period clothing:

  bonnet   cloak   neckerchief

  muff   cravat

- recipes and samples of food from the era:

  applesauce   apple pie   cornbread

  Johnny cakes   hardtack   cranberry pudding

- collections of accessories (or drawings, replicas, or models)

  apron   chisel   homemade cosmetics

  model ships   hornbook   homemade candle

  lantern   apothecary tools

- sharing of music or information about music in the era:

  fife music

  drums and the American Revolution

  classical music of the 1700's

One excellent source for this project was
http://www.history.org/index.cfm, a site about Colonial Williamsburg.

Be the Character! Rubric

Student _____ Date _____

Evaluator _____

Use this rubric to guide your work and preparation for presentation.
It can also be used for yourself, a peer, or the teacher to give
you feedback.

Student Handout

	Advanced 4	Proficient 3	Partially Proficient 2	Unsatisfactory 1
Planning Sheet	Fully completed with attention to detail and specific references to the text	Fully completed with specific references to the text	Mostly completed; missing some details	Incomplete or inaccurate
Accuracy	Includes accurate, specific, and thoughtful details from the text	Includes accurate details and some specific details from the text	Includes mostly accurate details from the text; includes some inaccuracies	Few accurate details; some or many inaccurate details
Visual Appeal	Wow!	Attractive and well done	Interesting; lacks detail or variety	Bland, uninteresting
Project	Elements are well done, unique, innovative, and creative	Elements are well done, creative	Most elements are well done; lacks attention to detail	Not well done; information or purpose not clear
Presentation	Presented in an organized way with enthusiasm, detail, and clarity	Presented in an organized way with clarity	Presentation lacked organization or clarity	Presentation lacked organization AND clarity

Total Score _____ **of 20**

Name _____ Date _____

Be The Character! Assignment Guide

Student Handout

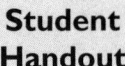

Your task is to choose a character from your reading and create a project or artifact that fits the character.

Step 1:

Think about your character and make some notes below. Not all topics will fit your specific character. Focus on the ones you know or can infer.

> The right costume makes the play!

- Clothing: What is unique about your character's clothing? How might it look?

- What special accessories does your character need for his or her life or work? (Examples: hat, shoes, lantern, saddle, musical instrument, tool, map, weapon, toy, doll, candle)

- What foods might your character eat?

- What music or dances might your character enjoy?

Step 2:

Choose your project. Consider the items above and decide on one for your project. Your project can be life-size or you can make a scale model if necessary—depending on the nature of the project and available materials. Do you want to design and make clothing? Or replicate or show an accessory? Or cook something for the class? Or play music your character might enjoy? Or teach the class a dance?

Continues on next page.

Name _____   Date _____

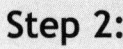

Be The Character! Assignment Guide, continued

Step 3: Plan!

- What character will serve as the inspiration for your project?

- What project will you create?

- How will it look or sound?
  (Draw a diagram at the bottom of the page, if possible.)

- What materials will you need?

- What research will you need to conduct to make your project as accurate as possible?

- How will you present your work to the class?

Student Handout

Draw a diagram of your project.

Name _____   Date _____

INTEGRATE ART WITH SET DESIGN

Type of text: Novels, short stories, biographies, poetry, drama, narrative nonfiction, articles, or any other nonfiction with an identifiable setting

Standards addressed: Standards related to: close reading of key ideas and details in a text; drawing inferences and conclusions; summarizing or paraphrasing; identifying setting and analyzing its role in a text; analyzing text structure as it relates to setting; integrating elements of a text; researching to build knowledge; translating information from text into visual form; gathering and presenting relevant information from multiple sources; taking notes; giving an oral presentation; presenting with multimedia components; conventions of standard English; and knowledge and use of language.

CCSS: ELA-Literacy.RL.6-8.1-3, 5, 7, 10; RI.6-8.1-3, 5, 7, 10; RH.6-8.1-2, 5, 7, 10; RST.6-8.1-2, 5, 7 10; W.6-8.4, 6-10; WHST.6-8.4, 6-10; SL.6-8.2, 4-6; L.6-8.1-3, 6

Approximate lesson time: Varies depending on requirements (minimum one class period)

Materials and preparation: Text; copies of student handouts, "Set Design Plan" (page 141) and "Set Design Rubric" (page 142); other materials dependent on the details of the assignment (may include paint, chalk, mural paper, construction paper, cardboard boxes, and/or other building materials)

Overview: This lesson helps students explore and understand the settings of a text and use visual arts to represent one setting.

Information for teachers: The amount of choice the students have in this lesson is up to the teacher. Students can design sets in a 2-D format by drawing, painting, or coloring (including using technology). They can also design and build sets in a 3-D format with a variety of supplies, including digital devices.

Where possible, find a place to display and share student constructions so that they can have a wider audience outside the classroom. For example, schedule a "Gallery Walk" in your school halls or media center to show off set designs.

Technology connections: Students may use a computer program to design and plan their set. It is also possible to make the set "construction" completely online if students are familiar with 3-D design tools. Students can also create virtual tours of their completed sets on video and share them online.

Strategies for differentiation: Because texts and settings within them vary in complexity, the lesson will automatically be differentiated when students choose their own texts and the setting they will feature. If this assignment is based on a class book or a book that's challenging for some students, additional scaffolding will be helpful. For example, the teacher can list some elements of the setting for the students or provide a fill-in-the-blank-type planning sheet.

Assessment: The "Set Design Rubric" on page 142 can serve as an evaluation tool to be completed by the teacher, peers, or the student.

Directions for students:

Step 1 **CHOOSE:** Select a scene from your text—one that is presented with several details.

Step 2 **ANALYZE:** Closely examine the setting of the scene you choose and identify its important components. Use the handout "Set Design Plan" to help you.

Step 3 **DESIGN:** Create a visual depiction of your set on paper or on computer or tablet. Be sure to include appropriate and accurate details from the text. Do any research you need to gain information for representation of the setting.

Step 4 **CONSTRUCT:** Build or otherwise create the set. Review the "Set Design Rubric" to understand how your project will be evaluated.

Step 5 **PRESENT:** Share your completed, constructed set with a group. Describe the importance of the setting to the text's meaning or message.

Examples:

Here are some examples of the kinds of settings middle-grades students used as the bases for their set designs.

From fictional texts:

- The house from "The Tell-Tale Heart" (Poe)
- The arena from *The Hunger Games* (Collins)
- Digitopolis or Dictionopolis from *The Phantom Tollbooth* (Juster)
- The drugstore from "Oranges" (Soto)
- The train track route and the train from "The Railway Train" (Dickinson)
- The French village of *The Rhinoceros* (Ionesco)
- The arena from "The Lady or the Tiger?" (Stockton)
- The Great Hall or the village of Huntercombe from *The Dark Is Rising* (Cooper)

From nonfictional texts:

- The attic from *The Diary of Anne Frank* (Frank)
- The camp from *Farewell to Manzanar* (Houston)
- A portion of the cathedral from *Cathedral: The Story of Its Construction* (Macaulay)
- The amusement park (or one of the rides) from *Math Zone* (Peterson and Henderson)
- The ancient Han dynasty burial chamber from *Treasures of Mawangdui* (Liu-Perkins)
- The ocean floor from *The Next Wave: The Quest to Harness the Power of the Oceans* (Rusch)
- The walking route from Selma, Alabama, to Montgomery, Alabama, from *Because They Marched* (Freedman)
- Jesse and Eric's apartment from *How Two Lost Boys Rode the Internet Out of Idaho* (Katz)

Set Design Plan

Title of the text you read:

Page(s) or chapter(s) on which your set is based:

Details about the **location** of your set:

Details about the **time period** of your set:

What materials will you need to create the set design?

What specific items will be in your set?

Will there be characters in your set? If so, tell about them:

Use the back of this paper to sketch your set. Remember, to receive an advanced score, your set needs to include several accurate and detailed items.

When you're finished, it's time to construct!

Name _____ Date _____

Set Design Rubric

Student _____ Date _____

Evaluator _____

Use this rubric to guide your work and preparation for presentation. It can also be used by a peer or the teacher to give you feedback.

Student Handout

	Advanced 4	Proficient 3	Partially Proficient 2	Unsatisfactory 1
Planning Sheet	Fully completed with attention to detail and specific references to the text	Fully completed with specific references to the text	Mostly completed; missing some details and/or references to the text	Incomplete or inaccurate
Accuracy of Set Details	Set includes many accurate details from the text	Set includes several accurate details from the text	Set includes some accurate details from the text	Set includes few accurate details from the text
Visual Appeal	Wow!	Attractive and well done	Interesting; lacks detail and/or variety	Bland, uninteresting
Set Elements	Elements are well constructed, unique, innovative, and creative	Elements are well constructed and creative	Most elements are well constructed; lacks variety or attention to detail	Not well constructed; lacks variety

Total Score _____ of 16

Name _____ Date _____

THE TALK SHOW

Type of text: Literature, particularly stories with multiple characters

Standards addressed: Standards related to: close reading of key ideas and details in a text; finding information; drawing inferences and conclusions; summarizing information; finding evidence from the text to support conclusions and analysis; character development and analysis; identifying and comparing points of view; asking questions about a text; taking notes; writing argumentative or informational text; listening skills; interviewing skills; giving an oral presentation; presenting and defending a position; conventions of standard English; and knowledge and use of language.

CCSS: ELA-Literacy RL.6-8.1-3, 6-8, 10; W.6-8.1-2, 4, 6, 9-10; SL.6-8.1-6; L.6-8.1-3, 6

Approximate lesson time: Two class periods (one for preparation and one for the activity)

Materials and preparation: Text; copies of student handouts "Talk Show Planner" (page 147) and "Talk Show Evaluation" (page 148); costumes or props for character role-playing

Overview: This lesson checks student comprehension while exploring and comparing points of view. It is also interactive and incorporates collaboration, drama, and presentation skills.

Information for teachers: The task in this lesson is for the class to role-play a talk show, with one student taking the role of host or moderator, other students taking the roles of various characters from the text, and the rest of the class taking the roles of the "studio audience" members able to ask questions of the characters. Teachers have much discretion here, including whether or not to have multiple hosts, how many characters to have "on stage" at a time, who can play the various roles, and how the questions are posed.

Information for teachers, continued:

The host's role is to ask questions, call on audience members for questions, ensure that all "characters" get a chance to speak, and move the show along. Determine which student or students will serve as the host (or moderator). If needed, the teacher can be the moderator for the first part of the talk show, then take volunteers to moderate.

Students might benefit from seeing a video of an interview or talk show (from YouTube or other source) before they prepare for their talk show.

One goal of the lesson is for students to devise questions of varying cognitive levels. As a part of this, students might be encouraged to ask questions that inspire the character to support and defend an action, a cause, or a belief. Another possible approach that encourages this is to have each group become an expert on one character (other than their own) and write 10 questions for just that character, applying the levels of Bloom's Taxonomy of the Cognitive Domain to be sure that the questions are of varying complexity.

Technology connections: The talk show can also be rehearsed and pre-recorded using technology. Another adaptation would be to have a "back channel" discussion among audience members using an online chat room during the show.

Arts connections: If time permits, students can create accessories, props, or costumes to enhance the character representation.

Strategies for differentiation: The various roles lend themselves to differentiation well. Students more advanced in comprehension, critical thinking skills, and acting skills make the best hosts. Students who have had difficulty reading and fully comprehending the text in all its complexity may be more comfortable asking questions as audience members rather than being on stage trying to accurately represent a character.

Assessment: Students can self-assess their work and the work of their groups using the standards-based evaluation sheet on page 148. The teacher can use students' scores or use the same scoring sheet to assess students or groups independently.

Directions for students:

Step 1 **COLLABORATE:** Discuss your assigned character with your group and pose practice questions to one another. Remember that the content of the "Talk Show" should be true to the story—including setting, plot, characters, and theme.

Step 2 **PLAN:** Complete the planning sheet as a group. Include a brief introduction of the character as well as (if relevant) wardrobe, speaking style, attitude, and other character traits.

Step 3 **QUESTION:** Work together to think of questions for each character that will be part of the talk show. Write two or three questions for each. Write at least two levels of questions—one that can be answered "yes" or "no" and others that take more thought and analysis from the character.

Step 3 **CHOOSE:** Select one person from your group to role play your character. The rest of you will be audience members prepared to ask questions of all characters.

Step 4 **THINK, ACT, QUESTION:** Start the show! The host should begin by asking the characters to introduce themselves. After that, characters will interact and ad-lib while the audience asks questions. Students who have taken on character roles need to portray their characters accurately. This includes the student making appropriate and realistic inferences in keeping with the character (e.g., when asked "What would you do if…").

Step 5 **EVALUATE:** Each individual should complete the "Talk Show Evaluation" form.

 **Example:** After reading the Depression-era novel *No Promises in the Wind* (Hunt 1970), a group of middle-level students planned and participated in a talk show. The main characters in the story are two brothers; other significant characters are family members and workers in a traveling carnival.

- In this case, the class was divided into seven groups, one for each character. Students were assigned to a "character group," so there was a "Joey group," a "Josh group," a "Stefan group," and so on.

- Each group filled out the planner together, including the list of questions to ask other characters. Then each group chose one group member who would represent its character on the talk show stage. The rest of the group members became part of the audience.

- The following day, students came prepared for their roles (including hats and simple costumes). The host kicked off the show; then the characters introduced themselves and talked to each other briefly on stage. After that, audience members posed prepared questions to each of the characters while the host moderated. Questions ranged from comprehension to application and evaluation:

  What was your first stop when you ran away?

  How did the birth of your brother Joey affect you?

  Why do you think your mom told you it was okay to run away?

  What part did your friendship with Howie play in your development?

  How did your pride affect events and choices in your life?

  What was the cause of your conflict with Joey?

  Did you really love Janey?

  How are you like your father?

Group Talk Show Planner

Text _____ Character _____

Group members _____

For this activity, your group will represent one character from the text. Talk about your character, complete this planning sheet, then choose one person to appear on the talk show. The rest of the group will be in the "audience" and will be responsible for asking questions of other characters during the show.

Student Handout

A. Make notes about the character's . . .

1. . . . age and physical appearance.

2. . . . home and favorite places.

3. . . . passions and things he or she cares deeply about.

4. . . . family situation.

5. . . . main goal in life.

6. . . . biggest problems, obstacles, and fears.

7. . . . biggest influences.

8. . . . greatest strengths and weaknesses.

B. Prepare an opening statement for your character to introduce himself or herself to the audience.

C. On the back of this sheet, write 10 (or more) questions you can ask the other characters during the show.

Name _____ Date _____

Talk Show Evaluation

Name _____ Character represented _____

Group members _____

Circle the number that best fits your group's work.

Use this scale:

4 = **advanced** (above and beyond requirements)

3 = **proficient** (met requirements)

2 = **partially proficient** (met some requirements)

1 = **unsatisfactory** (met less than 50% of requirements)

Student Handout

4	3	2	1	All members of our group were prepared for the show, having read the material.
4	3	2	1	We explicitly drew on our preparation by referring to evidence from the text to prepare our character and write questions.
4	3	2	1	We followed the rules for the show and knew our individual roles.
4	3	2	1	We posed questions that connected the ideas of different characters and responded to others' questions and comments with relevant evidence, observations, and ideas.
4	3	2	1	We acknowledged new information expressed by others, and, when warranted, qualified or explained our own views in light of the evidence presented.
4	3	2	1	Overall, this is how I would rate my participation in the talk show.

Here's what I did best:

This is what I'd like to improve about my performance:

Name _____ Date _____

HISTORICAL FICTION AND HISTORICAL FACTS

Type of text: Historical fiction and informational text

Standards addressed: Standards related to: close reading of key ideas and details in a text; determining theme or central ideas; drawing inferences and conclusions; analyzing character development, plot, theme, setting, events, and time periods; integrating elements of a text; researching using a variety of texts, including digital texts; comparing fictional and nonfictional portrayal of similar events or time periods; representing text comparisons with various media; writing informational or explanatory text; presenting a finished product; evaluating a project presentation; conventions of standard English; and knowledge and use of language.

CCSS: ELA-Literacy RL.6-8.1-3, 5-10; RI.6-8.1-3, 5-10; RH.6-8.1-2, 5-10; W.6-8.2, 4, 6-10; WHST.6-8.2, 4, 7, 10; SL.6-8.2-6; L.6-8.1-3, 6

Approximate lesson time: One to three class periods, depending on the level of research required

Materials and preparation: Texts; computers or other devices for research; copies of student handouts "Historical Fiction and Historical Facts" (pages 152-153) and "Historical Fiction and Facts Project Rubric" (page 154)

Overview: This lesson helps students understand historical fiction by comparing historical events in the fiction to actual historical events.

Information for teachers: The premise of this lesson is that students compare plot, setting, and characters from a work of historical fiction to events, places, and people from the actual time period or event. Finally, they construct their own product (such as a timeline, poster, or slide show) to present the comparison. The teacher can give the students the factual information and ask them to align the events appropriately with the story. Or students can research the real events, people, and places.

Note that this same approach can be used to compare science fiction and science facts.

Technology connections: Any of the student projects can be created and shared in various platforms online, including podcasts and social media.

Arts connections: Students can add illustrations or photography to enhance their timelines. They also can add music to slide shows or create animated timelines with online animation tools.

Strategies for differentiation: While some differentiation will occur with text choice, students can be provided with specific articles and websites to help structure their research. In addition, students who have difficulty with the task due to their reading or research skills can be given the basic information and asked to order it and construct the timeline.

Assessment: The "Historical Fiction and Facts Project Rubric" on page 154 can serve as an evaluation tool to be completed by the teacher. You might gather feedback from other students for rating the project's visual appeal and creativity portions of the rubric. Discuss the evaluation with the student.

Directions for students:

Step 1   **ANALYZE:** Examine and describe the basic parts of your historical fiction text. Use Part 1 of the handout, "Historical Fiction and Historical Facts," as a guide and place to record your analysis.

Step 2   **RESEARCH:** Use reliable sources to learn about the actual historical events. Use Part 2 of the handout as a research guide and place to record your research findings.

Step 3   **CONSTRUCT:** Design and construct a project that visually compares your information from the fictional and nonfictional sources side by side. This can be done as a poster, a timeline, an online slide show, or in some other format (check with the teacher). Use the rubric to guide your work.

Step 4   **PRESENT:** Find a way to present your project online or in the classroom.

Historical Fiction and Historical Facts, page 3

Example: Here's a sixth-grader's basic timeline comparing the novel *Number the Stars* (Lowry, 1989) and the Holocaust:

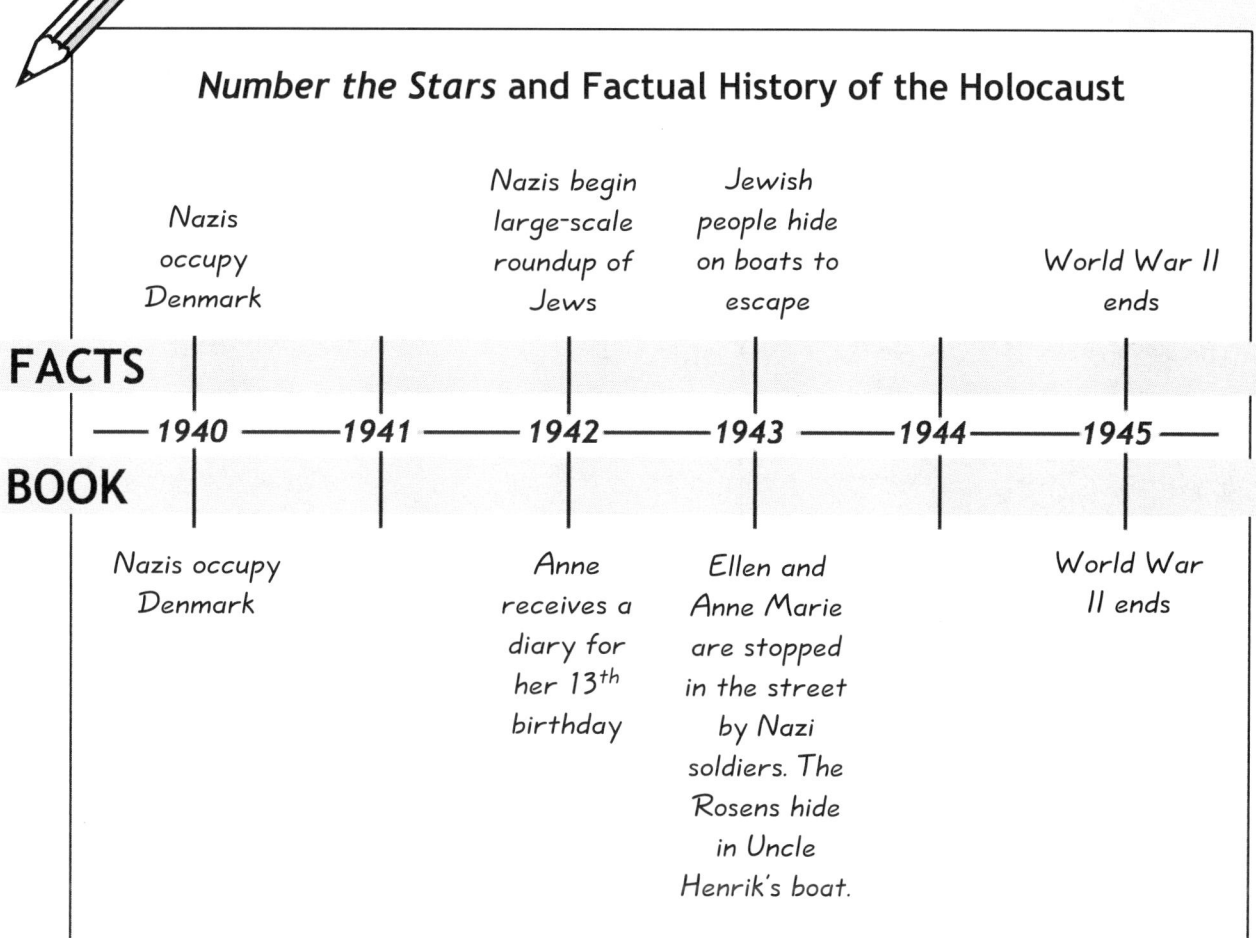

Number the Stars and Factual History of the Holocaust

FACTS

Nazis occupy Denmark

Nazis begin large-scale roundup of Jews

Jewish people hide on boats to escape

World War II ends

— 1940 —— 1941 —— 1942 —— 1943 —— 1944 —— 1945 —

BOOK

Nazis occupy Denmark

Anne receives a diary for her 13th birthday

Ellen and Anne Marie are stopped in the street by Nazi soldiers. The Rosens hide in Uncle Henrik's boat.

World War II ends

Use this same lesson to compare science fiction and scientific facts. A few examples of this are:

- Any of Jules Verne's science fiction books, comparing what Jules Verne predicted the future would be like and what it actually is like now

- The novel *1984*: comparing the story to the real 1984

- The movie: *2010: A Space Odyssey*: comparing the story to the real 2010

Historical Fiction and Historical Facts
Part 1: Analyze Historical Fiction

Use your text to fill in the information on this page.

Name _____ Date _____

Fiction title _____

Author _____ Year of publication_____

Characters: List all the important characters from the text.	**Plot:** List 10 memorable events from the plot of the text.
	1
	2
	3
	4
Setting: List as many times and places from the text as you can.	5
	6
	7
	8
	9
	10

Student Handout

Now go back and put an asterisk (*) by the events you feel might be real events from history (based on your own background knowledge).

Continues on next page

Name _____ Date _____

Part 2: Analyze Historical Facts.

Research the historical time period found in your text,
then fill in the information below.

Student Handout

People: List 10 people who were influential during the time period.

_____   _____

_____   _____

_____   _____

_____   _____

_____   _____

Places: List the places that played a significant role in this historical period.

Events and Dates: List five (or more) events from history that overlap with the event
that is the subject of your text. Include the dates.

Event	Date

Project: Now pull your information together and present it side-by-side. You can make a
poster, construct a timeline (on paper or online), or make a slide show. Here are
some websites that may help:
http://www.readwritethink.org/files/resources/interactives/timeline_2/
http://www.softschools.com/teacher_resources/timeline_maker/

Sources: Use the back of this page to list the sources you used to gather historical facts.

Name _____   Date _____

Historical Fiction and Facts Project Rubric

Student _____

Evaluator _____ Date _____

Student Handout

Scale:	Advanced 4	Proficient 3	Partially Proficient 2	Unsatisfactory 1
Story Analysis				
Plot	100% accuracy	80 to 99%	70 to 79%	Less than 70%
Setting	100% accuracy	80 to 99%	70 to 79%	Less than 70%
Characters	100% accuracy	80 to 99%	70 to 79%	Less than 70%
Historical Research				
People	100% accuracy	80 to 99%	70 to 79%	Less than 70%
Places	100% accuracy	80 to 99%	70 to 79%	Less than 70%
Events	100% accuracy	80 to 99%	70 to 79%	Less than 70%
Project				
Visual appeal	Fun to look at—WOW!	Fun to look at	Difficulty keeping audience's interest	Hard to see or understand
Accurate side-by-side comparison	100% accurate comparison	80 to 99% accurate comparison	70 to 79% accurate comparison	Less than 70% accuracy
Originality	Different and highly original	Different and original	Somewhat different	Ordinary and/or similar to many others

Total Score _____ of 36

Name _____ Date _____

RESPOND WITH A SONNET

Type of text: Literature or informational text

Standards addressed: Standards related to: close reading of key ideas and details in a text; determining and analyzing theme or central ideas; summarizing all or part of a text; drawing inferences or conclusions; analyzing the meaning or impact of certain text events, settings, or characters; relating themes, events, or experiences to real life events; comparing fictional and nonfictional accounts of an event or era; determining meanings of words or phrases as they are used in the text; writing informational or narrative text; producing clear and coherent writing; strengthening writing; engaging in collaborations and discussions; conventions of standard English; and knowledge and use of language.

CCSS: ELA-Literacy RL.6-8.1-4, 6-7, 10; RI.6-8.1-4, 6-8, 10; RH.6-8.1-4, 6-8, 10; RST.6-8.1-4, 6-8, 10; W.6-8.2-10; L.6-8.1-6

Approximate lesson time: 40 minutes

Materials and preparation: Text(s); copies of student handouts "Sonnet Assignment" (pages 158-159) and "Sonnet Feedback" (page 160); access to research materials (optional); discussion of sonnet prior to this lesson

Overview: For this lesson, students will write a sonnet based on a text they've read. Within that structure, however, students can have freedom to choose their topics or focus and the details they will include.

Information for teachers: A sonnet is a poem of expressive thought. Classical sonnets come in different forms, with differing rhyming patterns or no discernible rhyming pattern. However, most sonnets have 14 lines, 10 syllables in a line, and are written in iambic pentameter. (*Iambic pentameter* means a line consisting of five *iambs*. An iamb is a two-syllable foot in which the second syllable receives more stress than the first syllable. For example, the words *indeed, between,* and *mistake* form iambs.) For this lesson, the teacher may specify a certain form that students follow. A sonnet can be used to respond to virtually any topic or text in any subject. Encourage students to choose topics that pique their interest, curiosity, emotions, or passion.

Information for teachers, continued:

The sonnet assignment can relate to a specific text or group of texts, or it may be wide enough to allow students to choose any topic or text they have studied in the class or in a specified time span of the class.

Technology connections: Encourage students to do research on the Internet and type their final work for display. Students can also publish their sonnets on such a class website as Schoology® or Google Classroom™ or such an online bulletin board as Padlet™ or Pinterest®.

Arts connections: Students can mount, decorate, illustrate, and display their finished sonnets. Sonnets can be presented as a slide show with one line to a slide accompanied by art or music.

Strategies for differentiation: Students will automatically differentiate the assignment with their choice of texts or topics. You can differentiate the difficulty of the poetry writing by making rhyme optional and allowing for variance from the 10-syllable lines and from the iambic pentameter pattern.

Assessment: The teacher or peers can use the "Sonnet Feedback" form on page 160 to give evaluative feedback. This can also be used as a self-evaluative tool.

Directions for students:

Step 1   **REVIEW:** Think about the text or texts that you have read for this assignment. Review the topics, characters, ideas, and events.

Step 2   **RECALL:** Remember our discussion about sonnets. Remember that a sonnet is a poem that expresses thoughts and feelings. Recall which of the aspects of your text(s) elicited strong responses from you.

Step 3   **READ, PLAN, and WRITE:** Carefully read the details and directions on the "Sonnet Assignment" handout. Follow the steps to plan, write, and polish your sonnet.

Example: In both sonnets here, students used a 14-line format with three stanzas of four lines followed by a two-line stanza, lines as close to 10 syllables as possible. Rhyming and use of iambic pentameter were optional.

For one assignment, students in a science class studied the solar system and translated some of their understandings into sonnets (below, left).

Our Solar System
Joe, Grade 7

The sun's a blazing giant, stormy star
Takes center stage in our solar system
Hanging 93 million miles from Earth
Without the sun, no life is possible
Terrestrial planets, closest to the sun
Are mostly composed of iron and rock,
Valleys, craters, and molten metal cores
They are Mercury, Venus, Earth and Mars
Further from the sun are the gas giants
Four planets with no solid surfaces
Jupiter, Saturn, Uranus, Neptune
Basically hydrogen and helium
Earth alone is able to support life
At least, that is, as far as we now know…

The Holocaust
Christina, Grade 8

A Jewish nation being destroyed
Lives exterminated by the millions
Thousands of soldiers being deployed
Not knowing if they would ever return
Hoards of people, the smell of burning flesh
The heat, the horror of gas chambers
Ringing in your ears from a shot
    at the chest
Not knowing if you would be the next
The empty streets and eerie quietness
Nazis suddenly marching into the street
Dropping to your knees
    as they search your house
Praying they won't take anything,
    praying you won't die
This is the horror of the Holocaust
Never forget it; never forget it.

For another assignment, students in a social studies class were asked to synthesize ideas from a nonfiction article about World War II and from varying historical fiction stories with a World War II theme and put their thoughts and reactions into a sonnet (above, right).

SONNET ASSIGNMENT

Student Handout

Directions: Your task is to write a SONNET related to

(text) _____

Step 1: Choose a text (or more than one text related to the same general topic or idea).

Step 2: Brainstorm topics that are related to the text. List all the topics that spark your interest—anything about which you could express thoughts or give responses. Write these below.

Step 3: Circle the topic above that you like best.

Step 4: Gather details. Switch your brainstorming to your chosen topic. List as many descriptive words or phrases as you can think of that relate to the topic. Use all your senses. Also list subtopics, ideas, people, concepts, events, or settings that relate to your topic. You can include words that describe your thoughts, feelings, questions, or other responses to the topic.

Continues on next page

Name _____   Date _____

Sonnet Assignment, continued

Student Handout

Step 5: Write your sonnet. Put your ideas into a 14-line poem, following the form of three four-line sections plus a two-line ending. Make each line approximately 10 syllables long. *Rhyming is optional!* Try for iambic pentameter rhythm, but this too is optional. Write your rough draft here. Include lots of details. Use other paper if you need more drafts!

Section 1 _____

_____

_____

_____

Section 2 _____

_____

_____

_____

Section 3 _____

_____

_____

_____

Section 4 _____

_____

_____

Step 6: Edit and revise. Make sure it's just the way you like it, and be sure you've met all the requirements and done your best. Use the "Sonnet Feedback" rubric to guide your revision.

Step 7: When you are satisfied with the sonnet, type it up and hand it in. Be sure to include a title!

Name _____ Date _____

Sonnet Feedback

Name _____ Date _____

Related text(s) _____

Evaluator _____

Student Handout

Ideas   4   3   2   1
Clear main idea, interesting details; communicated writer's thoughts; ideas flow smoothly

Word Choice   4   3   2   1
Words are accurate, specific, appropriate, vivid, precise, and engaging

Organization   4   3   2   1
Includes three 4-line sections and a final 2-line section; each section represents an individual idea; entire sonnet fits together; attempts 10-syllable lines

Voice   4   3   2   1
Projects individual point of view and personal response to the topic; includes "poetic license" and unique perspective

Conventions   4   3   2   1
Nearly error free, accurate spelling and punctuation where necessary

Presentation   4   3   2   1
Final copy typed; shows pride in work

Key

4 = **advanced;** above and beyond requirements

3 = **proficient;** met requirements

2 = **partially proficient;** met some requirements

1 = **unsatisfactory;** met less than 50% of requirements

Total _____ of 24

Name _____ Date _____

MOVIE-BOOK COMPARISON

Type of text: Literature or informational text

Standards addressed: Standards related to: close reading of key ideas and details in a text; determining and analyzing theme and central ideas; summarizing a text; drawing inferences or conclusions; analyzing text structure; analyzing the meaning or impact of plot events, settings, or characters; comparing and contrasting written text with information or story presented in media or other format; writing informational or explanatory text; producing clear and coherent writing; effectively engaging in collaborations and discussions; conventions of standard English; and knowledge and use of language.

CCSS: ELA-Literacy RL.6-8.1-3, 5-7, 9-10; RI.6-8.1-3, 5-7, 9-10; RH.6-8.1-2, 5-6, 10; RST.6-8.1-2, 5-10; W.6-8.2, 4, 6-10; WHST.6-8.2, 4, 6-10; SL.6-8.1-6; L.6-8.1-3, 6

Approximate lesson time: Two to three class periods (depending on movie length)

Materials and preparation: Text (s); movie and accompanying book in numbers sufficient for students; copies of the three-page student handout "Movie-Book Comparison" (pages 164-166) and the student handout "Self Reflection on Movie-Book Comparison" (page 167)

Overview: For this lesson, students will compare a written and movie version of a text—analyzing the components of each and contrasting the two formats.

Information for teachers: This lesson works well with texts of any length and can easily be adapted for students of all ages. There are dozens of choices of movie-book combinations. (Remember to look for nonfiction works, too!) Don't hesitate to recommend books that might be at the lower end of a student's reading ability—as the experience of the comparison is rigorous and may go more smoothly on a first try with a book that is easy to read.

Preview any movie and read any book before making these available to students and assess them with the standards you would follow in reviewing any texts. If students are choosing individual book-movie combinations, parent permission might be a good idea.

Technology connections: Students can engage in a "back channel" chat during the movie using a site such as Graphite™ or TodaysMeet.com. During the chat, the teacher can introduce questions and the students can help each other with their responses while watching the movie.

Arts connections: This lesson lends itself well to a discussion of movie making. The students can analyze the decisions made by the movie's directors, including actor's portrayal of characters, visuals, sound effects, and music. Another way to connect visual arts is to ask students to design their own visual representations of the text before they see the movie. They can then compare their ideas to the ones used in the movie.

Strategies for differentiation: The choice of the book and movie allows the teacher to tailor this lesson to the student group. In addition, the teacher can give the handout "Movie-Book Comparison" with the book portions filled in to students who need an easier task. This helps every student finish the assignment and participate in the discussion.

Assessment: The "Movie-Book Comparison" handout itself can be assessed for completion and accuracy. Alternatively, the discussion can be the graded component of this assignment with students getting points according to the completeness and effectiveness of the way they support their opinions with evidence. In addition, students can use the self reflection form (page 167) to evaluate their own work on the assignment.

Directions for students:

Step 1   **READ:** Make sure you have completely read the assigned book.

Step 2   **WATCH:** Watch the movie version of the book.

Step 3   **WRITE:** Complete all portions of the 3-page "Movie-Book Comparison" handout.

Step 4   **DISCUSS:** Discuss the movie and book with classmates using your "Movie-Book Comparison" handout as a guide.

Movie-Book Comparison, page 3

Examples:  Here's a list of some of the many book-movie combinations that may be workable or appropriate for early adolescent students.

1984, George Orwell

Accidental Billionaires, Ben Mezrich (Movie: *The Social Network*)

Animal Farm, George Orwell

Anne Frank: The Diary of a Young Girl, Anne Frank

The Bad Beginning, The Reptile Room, and *The Wide Window*, Lemony Snicket (Movie: *A Series of Unfortunate Events*)

The Black Cauldron, Lloyd Alexander

The Black Stallion, Walter Farley

The Borrowers, Mary Norton

Bridge to Terabithia, Katherine Paterson

A Brief History of Time, Stephen Hawking

Charlie and the Chocolate Factory, Roald Dahl

The Chocolate War, Robert Cormier

David Copperfield, Charles Dickens

Derby Girl, Shauna Cross (Movie: *Whip It*)

Eragon, Christopher Paolini

Fahrenheit 451, Ray Bradbury

Fast Food Nation, Eric Schlosser

Flipped, Wendelin Van Draanen

The Giver, Lois Lowry

The Golden Compass, Philip Pullman

Great Expectations, Charles Dickens

Harry Potter and the Sorcerer's Stone, J. K. Rowling

Hatchet, Gary Paulsen (Movie: *A Cry in the Wild*)

The Hobbit, J. R. R. Tolkien

Holes, Louis Sachar

Hoot, Carl Hiaasen

The Hunger Games, Suzanne Collins

I, Robot, Isaac Asimov

The Incredible Journey, Sheila Burnford (Movie: *Homeward Bound*)

InkHeart, Cornelia Funke

James and the Giant Peach, Roald Dahl

Journey to the Center of the Earth, Jules Verne

Jumanji, Chris Van Allsburg

Jumper, Steven Gould

The Jungle Book, Rudyard Kipling

Jurassic Park, Michael Crichton

The Last of the Mohicans, James Fenimore Cooper

The Lightning Thief, Rick Riordan

The Lion, the Witch, and the Wardrobe, C. S. Lewis (Movie: *The Chronicles of Narnia: The Lion, the Witch, and the Wardrobe*)

Little Women, Louisa May Alcott

Lord Jim, Joseph Conrad

Lord of the Flies, William Golding

The Lord of the Rings, J. R. R. Tolkien

My Friend Flicka, Mary O'Hara (Movie: *Flicka*)

The Outsiders, S. E. Hinton

The Perfect Storm, Sebastian Junger

Peter Pan, J. M. Barrie

The Princess Bride, William Goldman

Queen Bees and Wannabes, Rosalind Wiseman (Movie: *Mean Girls*)

Seabiscuit: An American Legend, Laura Hillenbrand (Movie: *Seabiscuit*)

The Secret Garden, Frances Hodgson Burnett

Shiloh, Phyllis Reynolds Naylor

Stormbreaker, Anthony Horowitz

A Tale of Two Cities, Charles Dickens

The Time Machine, H. G. Wells

To Kill a Mockingbird, Harper Lee

Treasure Island, Robert Louis Stevenson

Tuck Everlasting, Natalie Babbit

The War of the Worlds, H. G. Wells

White Fang, Jack London

The Wizard of Oz, L. Frank Baum

A Wrinkle in Time, Madeleine L'Engle

Movie-Book Comparison

Name _____ Date _____

Book _____

Movie _____

Characterization

Student Handout

Name	Description in the book	Description in the movie	Noticeable differences	Static or dynamic?

Continues on next page

Name _____ Date _____

Movie-Book Comparison, page 2

Student Handout

Settings

	In the book	In the movie	Noticeable differences
Time(s)			
Place(s)			

Plot

	Major events or scenes in the book	Major events or scenes in the movie
Beginning		
Middle		
Climax		
End		

Continues on next page

Name _____ Date _____

Movie-Book Comparison, page 3

Theme

A. The **theme** of a text is the *message* the author is trying to give the reader about the subject matter of the text. In the space below, brainstorm possible *themes* from this text (book and movie versions).

B. Were there any themes that were in one format and not the other? If so, list them:

C. Now choose one theme you like and write it on the line. Below it, write evidence from the text of the book or movie that supports the theme.

Theme _____

_____

evidence

_____

evidence

_____

evidence

D. After everyone has had time to fill out this Movie-Book Comparison, discuss this question as a small group:

> *Which version of this text was better? Why? In the discussion, support your opinion with specific reasons.*

Name _____ Date _____

Self Reflection on Movie-Book Comparison

To compare two presentations of the same story or topic, it takes keen observation and sharp analysis of characters, settings, events, and themes. Use this page to reflect on the process and success of your comparison.

Student Handout

1. How thoroughly did I notice and record the importance of **characters** in the story (in both formats)?

2. How thoroughly did I notice and record the importance of **setting** to the story (in both formats)?

3. How thoroughly did I notice and record the importance of **themes** in the story (in both formats)?

4. How meaningful is the **evidence** I found (in one or both formats) to describe the theme?

5. What **biases or preconceived ideas** did I have in favor of or against one format (book or movie)?

6. What was my best **contribution** to the group discussion?

Name _____ Date _____

ALPHABET BOOK

Type of text: Literature and informational text

Standards addressed: Standards related to: close reading of key ideas and details in a text; determining and analyzing theme and central ideas; summarizing all or part or a text; determining meanings of words or phrases as they are used in the text; researching to build and present knowledge; gathering information from multiple sources; taking notes; synthesizing gathered information; using media as part of a presentation; writing informational or explanatory text; producing clear and coherent writing; strengthening writing; conventions of standard English; and knowledge and use of language.

CCSS: ELA-Literacy RL.6-8.1-4, 6-7, 10; RI.6-8.1-4, 6-7, 10; RH.6-8. 1-4, 6-7, 10; RST.6-8.1-4, 6-7, 10; W.6-8.2, 4, 6-10; WHST.6-8.2, 4, 6-10; L.6-8.1-6

Approximate lesson time: Two to three class periods

Materials and preparation: Text(s); copies of student handouts, "Alphabet Book Assignment" (page 172) and "Alphabet Book Rubric" (page 173); computer with Internet access for research and word processing

Overview: This lesson gives students a chance to synthesize what they have learned from their reading (including research) and apply it in a form that combines informative or explanatory writing with visual representation for an audience you determine ahead of time.

Information for teachers: The task is for each student to make one page of an ABC book focusing on an aspect of the text they have read. When all the pages are compiled, the class will have a complete book of text responses. See that all letters of the alphabet are used, if possible. Letters may be doubled if there are more than 26 students.

Technology connections: This project works equally well on paper or in electronic form. Many programs and apps are available to make online books, including Creative Book Builder™.

Arts connections: Illustration and design are part of creation of the alphabet page. In addition, students can translate their pages into slides—adding graphics created or found online.

Strategies for differentiation: Allowing students to self-select topics will help them choose a concept at their level of understanding. Additionally, students who have difficulty with research skills can be paired with better readers for the research. For students who find the writing of the alphabet page too challenging, the teacher can provide a page template for their work.

Assessment: A standards-based rubric is provided on page 173. This can be used for self-assessment, peer assessment, or final teacher assessment.

Directions for students:

Step 1 **CHOOSE and RECALL:** Choose a letter of the alphabet (unless one is assigned to you). Recall something from the text that starts with your letter. It could be an idea, event, setting, character, plot point, theme, vocabulary word, concept, or anything else appropriate.

Step 2 **RESEARCH:** Once you have chosen your letter and topic, research facts, definitions, details, quotations, and pictures or other graphics from both the text and other sources (books, websites, databases) about the topic.

Step 3 **DESIGN:** Use the "Alphabet Book Assignment" handout as a guide while you plan your page of the ABC book. Consider your audience as you design the layout of the page. Illustrations and graphics will make the page appealing.

Step 4 **WRITE:** Carefully write the informative portion of your page. Consult the rubric for guidance.

Step 5 **REVIEW and REVISE:** Make sure your work is free of mistakes, easy to understand, and looks the way you want it to look.

Step 6 **PUBLISH:** Contribute your page to the class ABC book.

Alphabet Book, page 3

Examples:

Text: *A Black Hole Is Not a Hole* by Carolyn Cinami DeCristofano

S is for Supermassive	Supermassive is the word used to describe the largest black holes—those that have a mass as great as 20 times the mass of the sun. Scientists believe that every large galaxy contains a supermassive black hole at its center. The Milky Way galaxy has a supermassive hole at its center. This has been named Sagittarius A. Scientists think supermassive holes were made at the same time as the galaxies that they are in.

Text: *Chew on This* by Eric Schlosser and Charles Wilson

J is for JUNK FOOD Junk food is food that is high in calories but low in nutritional value, such as foods, starchy breads, sweet drinks, and ice cream or other sugary desserts. A diet heavy in	junk food greatly contributes to type II diabetes, damage to the arteries, and obesity in children. The sugar, salt, and fats in junk food activate the brain and create a craving for more. Studies find that once a child eats fast food, she or he will eat fewer nutrients the rest of the day.

Text: *The Autobiography of Benjamin Franklin* by Benjamin Franklin

P is for <u>Poor</u> <u>Richard's Almanack</u>	<u>Poor Richard's Almanack</u> was an almanac published by Benjamin Franklin. It was a popular pamphlet sold throughout the American colonies from 1732 to 1738. The almanac brought success to Franklin. Many of the proverbs and aphorisms from the almanac still have popularity today.

Alphabet Book, page 3

Text: *Much Ado About Nothing* by William Shakespeare

C

is for

comedy

Comedy is a form of drama that has the purpose of amusing an audience. It is often fun and witty. A comedic drama generally ends with a joyful resolution to the conflict. Comedic performances often have the purpose of exposing foolishness or faults of people and social institutions and making fun of them with satire or parody (imitation).

Text: **"Hoods"** a poem by Paul B. Janeczko

H

is for hood

Hood is a shortened form of the word "hoodlum"—a slang term that began in Los Angeles, California,

in the 1980s. Initially it referred to a young street ruffian involved in crimes, especially someone belonging to a gang. Now the term also refers to a roughneck troublemaker—someone who behaves like a bully and is cruel or intimidating. Hoods often hang out with a group. This increases the intimidation.

Text: **"How to Play Drums—First Steps"** from www.howtoplaydrums.com

T

is for time signature

Time signature is a way to write rhythm (tempo) in music. It is written as a fraction at the beginning of a

piece of music to show the number and length of beats in each bar (measure). The numerator tells the number of beats in each bar (measure). The denominator shows the kind of note getting one beat. The most common time signature is 4/4 time. In 4/4 time, there are 4 beats in a measure. Each of them is a quarter note.

Alphabet Book Assignment

Student Handout

For this assignment, you will be making a page for a class alphabet book that is based on your reading in class.

A. Here are the goals for this project:

- Conduct a short research project related to a text you have read.
- Gather relevant information (research).
- Paraphrase and avoid plagiarism.
- Write explanatory text.
- Demonstrate command of the conventions of standard English.

B. Here are your steps for success:

- Draw a letter out of the basket.
- Choose the topic you want to feature on your ABC book page. (It needs to start with the letter you drew AND be directly related to the text).
- Research your term. Use the text plus any other resources (including online resources) to find information about your term.
- Design your page. It needs to include:
  - The letter and topic (example: *A is for Apprentice*)
  - A definition of the term followed by two or more sentences that explain the term and/or tie it to the text. (E.g., *An apprentice is someone who is learning a trade from an expert, usually for a set time period and low wages. Starting in 1731, Ben Franklin worked as an apprentice for his brother James. He was learning how to be a printer.*)
  - Include pictures, illustrations, or graphics that go with the topic.

Name _____   Date _____

Alphabet Book Rubric

Name _____ Your letter is _____

Evaluator _____ Date _____

Use the back of this paper to list the texts you read.

Student Handout

A = advanced   **P** = proficient
PP = partially proficient   **U** = unsatisfactory

	A	P	PP	U
RESEARCH PROCESS: Gather relevant information, take notes, cite sources accurately, and paraphrase.				
IDEAS: Explain topic with interesting and accurate information; include appropriate graphics to enhance the topic.				
ORGANIZATION: Develop the topic with relevant, well-chosen facts, definitions, concrete details, quotations, or other information and examples.				
WORD CHOICE: Use precise language and domain-specific vocabulary to inform about or explain the topic.				
FLUENCY: Use words, phrases, and clauses to create cohesion and clarify the relationships among ideas, facts, reasons, and evidence.				
CONVENTIONS: Use spelling, punctuation, and grammar correctly.				
PRESENTATION: Page is easy to read, appealing, and original. Teaches the topic in a unique and compelling way.				

Name _____ Date _____